Healing Your Soul

Don't Let Your Past Hurts Destroy Your Future

Greg and Sandy Burkett, Ph.D.
Patti Hathaway, M.Ed., CSP

Healing Your Wounds: Don't Let Past Hurts Destroy Your Future

By Greg and Sandy Burkett, Ph.D. and Patti Hathaway, M.Ed., CSP

Published By:
Breakthrough Hope & Healing
Westerville, Ohio
USA

ISBN: 978-0-9904763-2-0

Library of Congress Cataloguing-in-Publication Data
Hathaway, Patti
Burkett, Greg and Sandy

Healing Your Wounds: Don't Let Past Hurts Destroy Your Future

Healing
Your Soul

Don't Let Past Hurts Destroy Your Future

(A eight-session Bible Study for 1:1 and small groups)

www.BreakthroughHopeHealing.com

Name_____

Healing Your Soul Lessons

Introduction & Overview

This book was co-authored and published in 2010. With 10 years of experience using this content, I wanted to expand it to include two more lessons on Soul Ties and In Utero Trauma. I have found those topics to be critical for ministry with human trafficking victims, homeless people, and others impacted by past trauma of all sorts. I also added my own and others' personal stories at the beginning of each chapter. I find we learn so much as we share stories with each other and I hope this Bible Study inspires you to do your own soul healing. I welcome your stories of change as a result of this book. Please email them to me at GoHeal4God@protonmail.com.

Many blessings on your healing journey, Patti

In 1980, the Lord began to speak to my heart that few Christians understood how to minister to the hearts of individuals. Most individuals share with their friends, family, church leaders, and pastors before they go to a professional. Out of that need, Breakthrough Biblical Counseling training was birthed. The two-year course is designed to teach believers how to pray and support individuals through the healing of life wounds. The Breakthrough Living Bible Study series is designed for graduates to minister in small groups the healing power of Jesus Christ. We pray that during your journey of discovery that you will become empowered to reach your fullest potential through Christ Jesus.

Dr. Sandy

This Bible Study starts off with the core foundational lesson on *Understanding Your Body, Soul, and Spirit.* You will learn where sin lies so that you can break through your sin patterns and begin the process of healing your wounds. This lesson will teach you how to take the understanding and knowledge from your head to your spirit for true-life change. *Transformational Healing of In Utero Trauma* (Lesson Two) is where our journey begins before we are even born.

Once that foundation is set, you will break free from the wounds that you have control over in the next three lessons. Lesson Three will teach you *Who Own This Problem?* God wants you to understand the problems that affect your own inner healing because other peoples' problems cannot be owned or healed by you.

Lesson Four, *Breaking Your Inner Vows,* will teach you the importance of your own words and the impact they can have on your life. Enjoy newfound freedom by breaking your inner vows and living more freely in Christ. In Lesson Five you will learn how to *Gain Freedom from Bitter Root Judgments.* You may not realize that it may be your own judgments that prevent others from blessing you. In this lesson you'll learn how to release your Bitter Root Judgments in order to positively change your personal relationships.

The final three lessons will deal with wounds that have been caused by others. In Lesson Six, *When Others Curse You Intentionally or Unintentionally,* you will learn how to break the curses that have been spoken over you (intentionally or unintentionally) as well breaking those curses that you have spoken over others. In Lesson Seven, you will learn how to gain *Freedom Beyond Generational Limits/Curses.* This will address curses that existed before you were born. You may have been drawn to certain sins and never understood why. In this lesson you will learn why and how to have victory over generational strongholds. In Lesson Eight, we address the *Breaking Unhealthy Soul Ties that Bind You* in a powerful lesson that is sure to address past traumas.

At the end of each lesson is your own personal space for notes on your healing progress from each lesson.

Authors

Sandy Burkett, Ph.D. is the founder of Breakthrough Reconciliation Ministries. She has written and taught Breakthrough Biblical Counseling since 1988. Dr. Sandy has been in ministry since 1980. She counsels, equips, writes and speaks at conferences and churches throughout the United States and internationally. Dr. Sandy is recognized for her understanding of healing process of trauma, restoring joy and prophetic giftings. She is ordained through Christian International and has her Ph.D. from Trinity Theological Seminary, Newburgh, Indiana. Dr. Sandy's Ph.D. research was on *Restoring Joy in Victims of Childhood Trauma.* Her passion is help wounded individuals walk out the fullness of their destiny with joy.

Greg Burkett is an author and teacher of Breakthrough Biblical Counseling. Since 1990, Greg has joined Dr. Sandy in the ministry of equipping, teaching at conferences and churches nationally and internationally. Greg is recognized for his prophetic giftings and insight into family brokenness. Greg is ordained through Christian International under Bishop Bill Hamon. Greg's passion is to help individuals understand the healing process of their heart in order for their destiny to be released or restored.

Patti Hathaway, M.Ed, CSP is the author of seven books that have collectively sold over 100,000 copies worldwide. A Certified Speaking Professional who is known for her passion and personal stories, Patti is the 2010 Breakthrough Biblical Counseling graduate of the year. She is blessed to use her 20+ years of speaking and writing experience to partner with the Burketts to bring their life changing information to others. Patti is known for being a dynamic and inspirational speaker who will activate people to break through barriers with Jesus, the Living Word. She is an expert and author in change, customer service, leadership, and interpersonal communication skills. Her six eLearning programs deliver information in a unique format that changes how people think and act.

Acknowledgements

We would like to thank thousands of Breakthrough Biblical Counseling graduates over the years who have encouraged (and even pushed) us to write this Bible Study. We look forward to hearing many breakthrough stories as you teach others about the life-changing goodness of God's grace and redemption in healing wounds. A special thanks to Pat Masucci who piloted these materials in the Ohio Reformatory for Women and in a home Bible Study. Thank you Pat for your teaching insights and godly wisdom.

From Patti on the revised edition: I want to thank Alley Vedock for her editing on the nearly 100 pages of content I added to this edition. She is an encourager who inspires me to be my best self.

Understanding Your Body, Soul, and Spirit

For the first 45 years of my life, I was a wimpy Christian. Maybe I was a Pharisee – looking good on the outside but not so great on the inside?

I was a preacher's kid so I had to look perfect on the outside but my heart wasn't always in it.

I knew a lot of Scripture in my head but it hadn't gotten in to my spirit.

It reminds me of my youngest son Drew in his first year of playing football. He played scared and tried to avoid getting hit. It hurt! What happens when you play passive and scared? You get hurt more often.

Finally Drew made the decision that he had enough of being pushed around and living in fear. He got mad and he made the decision he wasn't going to take it anymore. He became more aggressive and hit players before they hit him. He was a much better player and became a team captain on many sports team after he learned that lesson.

When it comes to the game of life, as Christians we must learn to overcome the lies and intimidation of the devil.

It all comes down to understanding how to empower our spirit to control our body and soul. This is a foundational lesson that many do not understand. So let's get started...

I t is crucial to understand the difference between your body, soul, and spirit. In this foundational chapter, you will learn where sin lies so that you can break through your sin patterns and then begin the process of healing your inner wounds (which we will learn in later lessons). This lesson will teach you how to take your understanding and knowledge from your head to your heart for true-life change. God wants us to have victory over our sin by following His pattern for our life.

1. You were created in the _____ of the triune God. Your God is one God, yet He reveals Himself to people in **three** separate yet totally unified ways:
    a. God the Father
    b. God the Son who is Jesus the Christ
    c. God the Holy Spirit.

> *"For there are three that bear record in heaven, the Father, the Son, and the Holy Spirit: and these three are one."*
>
> **I John 5:7** (King James Version)

2. You were also created in a similar manner as **three** distinct yet unified parts that together make up one person.

Healing Your Soul

> *"And God said, Let us make man in our own image, after our own likeness."*
>
> **Genesis 1:26** (American Standard Version)

> *"See the Word of God is alive! It is at work and is sharper than any double edge sword. It cuts right through to where <u>soul</u> meets <u>spirit</u> and <u>joints meet marrow (body)</u>, and it is quick to judge the inner reflections and the attitudes of the heart. Before God nothing is hidden, but all things are naked and open to the eyes of Him to whom we must render account."*
>
> **Hebrews 4:12-13** (Complete Jewish Bible)

God created you with a _____, a _____, and a _____.

| Body/Flesh | Soul | Spirit |

3. **Body = World-Consciousness**: *"And the Lord God formed man's body from the dust of the ground."*

    Genesis 2:7

    a. Your body functions through the five senses of _____, _____, _____, _____ and _____. Your body allows you to experience the world around you.

b. Your body is also referred to as your _____.
Your flesh has its own desires, wants and needs, and
can exercise much control over you.

> *"Now may the God of peace Himself sanctify you
> completely, and may your whole **spirit, soul, and
> body** be preserved blameless at the coming of our
> Lord Jesus Christ."*
>
> **1 Thessalonians 5:23** (New King James Version)

4. **Soul = Self-Consciousness** *"and man became a living
soul"*   Genesis 2:7

a. Your soul consists of your mind, will, and your emotions. It is where your personality is formed.
1) The mind consists of your memory, _____,
and imagination.
2) The will is where you make decisions. It is where
you have the power to _____.
3) The emotions are where your _____ reside
(joy, anger, fear, depression…)

b. Your soul stands between your spirit and body, binding the two together. Your soul makes it possible for
your spirit and body to communicate.

5. **Spirit = God-Consciousness** *"and breathed into him
the breath of life."*   Genesis 2:7

a. Your spirit connects you to God's _____ and
it is through your spirit that you communicate with
God.

b. Your spirit is that part of you that is able to have a
_____ with Him.

c. Your spirit gives you life. It is your spirit that becomes new when you are born-again not your body
or your soul.

Healing Your Soul

> *"God is a spirit: and they that worship Him must worship Him in spirit and truth."*
>
> **John 4:24** (New American Standard Version)

6. **The Power of Your Soul**

   a. Your soul makes it possible for your spirit and the body to _____ and to cooperate with each other.

   b. When your soul is wounded or is strong willed, it _____ the person.

   c. When your spirit is strong in _____ _____, it will bring your body into subjection to the spirit through your soul. One of the functions of a healthy soul is to keep the body and the spirit of a person in their proper order according to the Word of God.

> God tells us *"For as he thinks in his heart so he is."*
>
> **Proverbs 23:7** (American King James Version)

The Hebrew word translated to "heart" in this passage is the word **nephesh** {neh´ fesh}. In the Old Testament this word was translated to soul 475 times, to life 117, times and to heart 15 times. *Strong's Lexicon* defines nephesh as *"the soul; the inner being of man; the man himself; the seat of appetites, emotions and passions; activity of the mind; activity of the will"*.

7. **How Do Trauma/Wounds/Curses Impact Your Soul?**
   a. Trauma/wounds/curses lead to negative thoughts because satan _____ to you.
   b. Sin always begins with a _____. You think about something and then you act on it. Your emotions begin with a thought. You cannot feel before you think. *It is your thoughts (your mind) that determine how you feel that influence your choices and what you decide to do (your will).*

ROOTS	FRUIT
	determine	*influences*
Your Thoughts →	**How You Feel** →	**What You Do**
(Mind)	(Emotions)	(Will/Choices)
satan lies to you		*impacts your*
SEED		
(Trauma/Wounds/Curses)		Circumstances

It's important to heal your SEED which comes from trauma, wounds, and curses. You then can change your ROOTS (thoughts) by breaking the power of the lies of satan and renewing your mind with the Truth from God (Romans 12:2). As a result, your FRUIT (how you feel and what you do) will change.

8. **The Functions of Your Spirit** — Your spirit cannot by itself act upon your body. It can only do so through your soul.

> *"My soul magnifies the Lord, and my spirit has rejoiced in God my Savior".*
> **Luke 1: 46-47** (NKJV)

Since your spirit communicates with God, you must be able to recognize whether you are being controlled by your body, soul, or spirit. Otherwise you will try to commune with God through your soul by using your intellect and feelings instead of the Holy Spirit.

We can find the personal spirit spoken of many times in scripture, including:

- Proverbs 25: 28 refers to *"his own spirit"*

- 1 Corinthians 5: 4; 14: 4 *"my spirit"*

- 1 Corinthians 2: 11 *"the spirit of the man which is in him"*

- Job 32: 8 *"there is a spirit in man"*

- Zechariah 12: 1 states that *"the Lord...formed the spirit of man within him"*

a. **Conscience** is the _____ ability to determine right from wrong by which you judge the moral character of others. The work of the conscience is direct and does not bend to outside opinion. A good conscience is a way of personal protection to keep you out of trouble—not merely to make you aware of sin.

> *"To the pure all things are pure: but to them that are defiled and unbelieving nothing is pure; but both their mind and their **conscience** are defiled."*
> **Titus 1:15** (NKJV)
> **(Other verses: Romans 2:15; John 8:9)**

b. **Communion** is defined as _____. Your personal spirit enables you to commune and to communicate with God, and to hear God. You commune with God in worship through your spirit not your soul. God is Spirit and can only be known intimately through your redeemed spirit.

> *"The true worshipers will **worship** the Father **in spirit and truth**".*
>
> **John 4:23** (NKJV)
>
> **(Other verses: I Corinthians 10:16; 2 Corinthians 13:14)**

9. **How Do You Feed Your Soul?** Your soul needs to be fed and nourished with good things, just as a growing child should be fed three balanced meals a day. The absence of these good things can starve and actually _____ your soul.

   a. Some good things that nourish (or lack thereof starve) your soul include:
      * Affection
      * Beauty
      * Laughter
      * Fellowship and Family
      * Music
      * Cherishing our own person

   b. We all have suffered some degree of woundedness. _____ wounds your soul. The absence of what is _____ also wounds your soul. A wounded soul can affect your walk with Christ and stop you from fulfilling your destiny. When your soul is wounded it can actually imprison your spirit.

   c. Your spirit may be ready to move ahead, but your wounded soul can hold you back. You need the _____ _____ of Jesus Christ in order to fulfill your destiny in God's kingdom and to walk in His freedom as overcomers!

10. Today we still deal with the struggle and the consequences of sin. Before you are born again, your spirit is _____ and _____ from God because of sin. Healing the wounds of your life will heal your soul. This process can only begin when you receive Jesus Christ as your personal Savior and Lord.*

*If you have not received Jesus as your Lord and Savior, please read the bonus materials on pages 123-128 for a complete explanation on salvation.

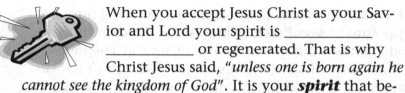 When you accept Jesus Christ as your Savior and Lord your spirit is _____ _____ or regenerated. That is why Christ Jesus said, *"unless one is born again he cannot see the kingdom of God"*. It is your **spirit** that becomes new, **not your soul** and **not your flesh**. Once you are saved you have the ability to change. Without God, you can only struggle to change through self.*

Prayer: *God help me keep my spirit pure and untangled by my flesh and soul. I want to be led by your Spirit and I ask that you daily fill my spirit with your Holy Spirit. In Jesus Name. Amen.*

> *"The sacrifices of God are a broken spirit; a broken and contrite heart—These, O God, You will not despise."*
>
> **Psalm 51:17** (NKJV)

*For information on the in-filling of the Holy Spirit, please read pages 129-131.

11. We need to address the importance of _____ in the process of healing our soul. In almost every prayer that we have in this book, we include forgiveness.

Whether it's an argument or long-held resentment toward a family member or friend, unresolved conflict can go deeper than you realize—it may be affecting your physical health. It's interesting that 62% of American adults say they need more forgiveness in their personal lives, according to a survey[1]. The good news? Even medical studies have shown that the act of forgiveness can reap huge rewards for your health, lowering the risk of heart attack; improving cholesterol levels and sleep; and reducing pain, blood pressure, and levels of anxiety, depression and stress. And research points to an increase in the forgiveness-health connection as you age[2].

"There is an enormous physical burden to being hurt and disappointed," says Karen Swartz, M.D., director of the Mood Disorders Adult Consultation Clinic at The Johns Hopkins Hospital. Chronic anger puts you into a fight-or-flight mode, which results in numerous changes in heart rate, blood pressure and immune response. Those changes increase the risk of depression, heart disease and diabetes, among other conditions. Forgiveness calms stress levels, leading to improved health[2].

Forgiveness is not just about saying the words. It's an active process in which you make a conscious decision to release your negative feelings towards another and give the pain it caused you to Jesus. You choose by an act of your will to forgive another. It's a divine exchange. Just as you gave Jesus your sin in exchange for His forgiveness (i.e. salvation), in this divine exchange you will forgive the other person (or yourself) and give Jesus your pain. Then ask Jesus what He will give you in exchange for your pain – it's always something better.

Sample prayer: *In the name of Jesus Christ I confess that I have not forgiven:___<name>___for___<act>___. The pain this situation has caused me is_____. I release and give to You Jesus all my pain. I make the choice by an act of my will to forgive_____<name>___.who hurt me. I ask you Jesus, please forgive me for not forgiving them. I break the power of this unforgiveness and offense over my life in the name of Jesus Christ and I sever it with the Sword of the Spirit. I renounce any demonization that exists as a result of my unforgiveness. Jesus, what will You give me in exchange for my pain?* (listen to what Jesus tells you because His sheep hear His voice, John 10:27). I receive

_____<what you heard>_____. I release___<name>___from my offense and I ask You to bless them and bless me as I choose to move on. I can walk this out in the name and power of Jesus Christ. Amen!

Forgiving yourself may be the hardest of all. Understand that people make mistakes and sometimes even intentionally choose the wrong way. But God's love for you is overwhelming and covers a multitude of errors. Stop punishing yourself and thinking you "deserve" this sickness. *He does not treat us as our sins deserve or repay us according to our iniquities. For as high as the heavens are above the earth, so great is His love for those who fear Him; as far as the east is from the west, so far has He removed our transgressions from us* (Psalm 103:10-12). Substitute yourself in the prayer provided and pray yourself through the forgiveness process.

Bitterness is a lot like a match, it only burns the person holding on to it. When ministering healing prayer, I've found that often unforgiveness blocks a person's healing. The Bible has a lot to say about forgiveness:

> *Get rid of all bitterness, rage and anger, brawling and slander, along with every form of malice. Be kind and compassionate to one another, forgiving each other, just as in Christ God forgave you.*
> **Ephesians 4:31-32**

> *And when you stand praying, if you hold anything against anyone, forgive them, so that your Father in heaven may forgive you your sins.*
> **Mark 11:25**

> *And forgive us our debts, as we also have forgiven*
> *our debtors. And lead us not into temptation, but*
> *deliver us from the evil one. For if you forgive other*
> *people when they sin against you, your heavenly*
> *Father will also forgive you.*
>
> **Matthew 6:12-14**

> *Bear with each other and forgive one another*
> *if any of you has a grievance against someone.*
> *Forgive as the Lord forgave you.*
>
> **Colossians 3:13**

If unforgiveness is a long-standing issue with you, I strongly recommend you seek deep soul healing and deliverance. There are people gifted to do this work. I can give you references if you email me.

12. There is one final tool I'd like to share that we will use throughout this book. It's called The _____ Exchange.

Ask Holy Spirit to show you what you need to give up to Him in exchange for something better. Just as you accepted Jesus as your personal Savior when you gave Him your sins in exchanged for your salvation.

When it comes to dealing with hurts and trauma you can do a divine exchange by saying: *Jesus I give to you* (list what pain, trauma, negative feeling, situation, etc.). Put it in your hands and then literally lift it up and give it to Jesus. Put your hands down when you feel you've given it to Him. Then say, Jesus, what will you give me in exchange for this? I recommend journaling what you are giving Jesus and what He gave you in exchange for future reference.

Breakthrough Declarations

At the end of each lesson, you will have a list of Biblical Declarations* that you say out loud to get the lesson concepts deep into your soul. *"Death and life are in the power of the tongue and those who love it will eat its fruit"* (Proverbs 18:21 NKJV).

When you combine prayers and declarations you become more intentional about the power of words. In Romans 4:17 TPT it states *"For in God's presence he believed that God can raise the dead and call into being things that don't even exist yet."* Declarations are a tool to help you align your faith and create a soul full of hope and courage even though you don't see it in the natural yet. These declarations can become weapons to change who you are in Christ.

1. I have the mind of Christ (1 Corinthians 2:16; Romans 12:2).

2. I am dead to sin and alive to obeying God (Romans 6:11).

3. I walk in ever-increasing health (Isaiah 53:3-5; Psalms 103:1-3).

4. I set the course of my life with my declarations (James 3:2-5).

5. God is on my side; therefore I declare that I cannot be defeated, discouraged, depressed or disappointed (Romans 8:37; Psalm 91; Philippians 4:13).

* Some declarations used with permission of Steve and Wendy Backlund with IgnitingHope.com

Fill-in-the-Blank Answer Guide

1. image
2. body
   soul
   spirit
3. a. seeing, hearing, taste, smell, touch
   b. flesh
4. a. 1) reasoning   2) choose   3) feelings
5. a. spirit
   b. relationship
6. a. communicate   b. controls   c. Christ Jesus
7. a. lies   b. thought
8. a. discerning   b. fellowship
9. wound
   b. trauma   good
   c. healing power
10. wounded   separated   born again
11. forgiveness
12. Divine

Resources

Research Facts about Forgiveness and Health pdf at:
http://releasenow.org/research

(1) http://fetzer.org/resources/fetzer-survey-love-and-forgiveness-american-society

(2) Research from: https://www.hopkinsmedicine.org/health/healthy_aging/healthy_connections/forgiveness-your-health-depends-on-it.

The Art of Forgiving by Lewis Smedes.

A More Excellent Way by Henry Wright.

Feelings Buried Alive Never Die by Karol Truman.

Contend for your Healing by Patti Hathaway

Healing In Utero Trauma

I'm a recovering workaholic. I've been driven to succeed since I was a little girl but never really knew why. I was an athlete in high school and played basketball and did field events for track. I was a singer. I sang in the Children's Bible Hour choir as a kid and was voted best singer in my high school graduating class.

As a senior in college, I was prescribed muscle relaxants due to stress. I went on to earn my Masters degree at The Ohio State University. I started my own speaking business and earned my Certified Speaking Professional designation at the age of 34. I was one of only 70 women worldwide to do so at the time. I authored five business books and by <u>all</u> outward appearances I was very successful.

Yet, there was such sadness at the <u>core</u> of who I was. I'd been a Christian most of my life (my father was a minister) and yet I didn't have deep joy in my life. I never truly felt loved. And, I

---

had built a wall around my heart so I wouldn't get hurt.

Thenl I attended a workshop on In Utero Trauma and discovered the root cause for my workaholism.A memory came back to me when I was about 10 years old. My mom excitedly came home and exclaimed that she just learned that the pills that many women took while she was pregnant with me to prevent a mis-carriage caused birth defects.

She didn't take the meds even though she was bleeding. As an adult, I can see why she didn't take the meds because my sisters and I were born within four years of each other. But as a 10-year-old, I took that in my heart to mean that she never really wanted me. That's why I didn't belong and never would. Ultimately, it's why I put up my performance wall—to earn my mother's love—but it was just never enough. My mom had her own abandonment issues and loved me the only way she knew how.

What I share in this chapter changed my life forever. And the In Utero trauma healing prayer time with Pat, my spiritual mentor, paved the way to change. And the same can be true for you as you apply this information to your own life. Seek Holy Spirit to uncover what trauma or wound may have been caused before you were even born.

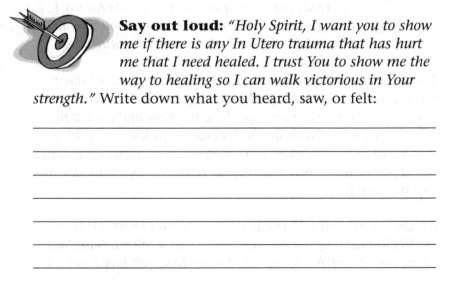 **Say out loud:** *"Holy Spirit, I want you to show me if there is any In Utero trauma that has hurt me that I need healed. I trust You to show me the way to healing so I can walk victorious in Your strength."* Write down what you heard, saw, or felt:

_____

_____

_____

_____

_____

_____

_____

1. God created each of you wonderfully and uniquely. The shaping of your _____ and _____ began in your mother's womb. What happens to all of us in the first nine months of our life between conception and birth molds and shapes our personalities, drives and ambitions in important ways. Psalms 139:13-16 from the Complete Jewish Bible shares clearly God's intention at the moment the sperm and egg meet.

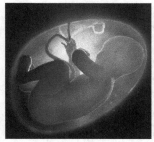

"For you fashioned my inmost being,
You knit me together in my mother's womb.
I thank you because I am awesomely made,
Wonderfully; your works are wonders-
I know this very well.
My bones were not hidden from You when I was being made in secret,
Intricately woven in the depths of the earth.
Your eyes could see me as an embryo,
But in your book all my days were already written;
My days have been shaped before any of them existed."

2. The Bible teaches that the life of a person begins at conception and science backs up this belief. During the months you were in your mother's womb, your mother was your conduit to the world. Everything that affected her affected you. How your mother viewed the _____ influenced how you view the world. The beliefs, judgments, and experiences your mother had while carrying you in her womb affected the very core of your _____.

3. Frank Lake, M.D., author of *Mutual Caring,* believes that the first three months of embryonic development are the most _____ part of one's life. Lake's research was based on the scriptures that express that fetal life:

- *Job 33:4 The Spirit of God has made me; the breath of the Almighty gives me life.*
- *Psalm 22:9-10 Yet you brought me out of the womb; you made me trust in you even at my mother's breast. From birth I was cast upon you; from my mother's womb you have been my God.*
- *Psalm 27:10 My father and mother abandoned me. I'm like an orphan! But you took me in and made me yours.*
- *Psalm 58:3 Wicked wanderers even from the womb, that's who you are! Lying with your words, your teaching is poison.*
- *Luke 1:41 At the moment she heard Mary's voice, the baby within Elizabeth's womb jumped and kicked. And suddenly, Elizabeth was filled to overflowing with the Holy Spirit!*
- *Luke 1:44 As soon as the sound of your greeting reached my ears, the baby in my womb leaped for joy.*
- *Eph. 2:10 We have become his poetry, a re-created people that will fulfill the destiny he has given each of us, for we are joined to Jesus, the Anointed One. Even before we were born, God planned in advance our destiny and the good works we would do to fulfill it!*

4. Trauma may begin as early as _____. If the sexual act in which a baby is conceived is hostile, fearful, ambivalent or just for a good time with no commitment on the part of the adults, both the egg and the sperm carry that cellular imprint of conception (*Imprint for Life* by Leah LaGoy).

5. Life in the _____ is remembered. The moment we are conceived we begin to store up treasures and/or traumas in our heart. Those treasures/traumas are made up of the attitudes, judgments (inner vows, bitter root judgments) and expectations we hold.

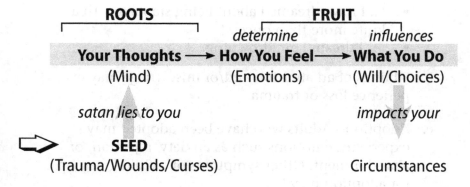

ROOTS   **FRUIT**

determine   *influences*

Your Thoughts ⟶ **How You Feel** ⟶ **What You Do**
(Mind)   (Emotions)   (Will/Choices)

satan lies to you   *impacts your*

⟹ **SEED**
(Trauma/Wounds/Curses)   Circumstances

- *Psalm 109:22 states "I'm so broken, needy and hurting. My heart is pierced through and I'm so wounded." A person who has been deeply wounded in utero will express that woundedness as child, adolescent, and adult.*
- *Job 32:8 (Amplified Bible) "But there is (a vital force) a spirit (of intelligence) in man, and the breath of the Almighty gives men understanding."* The woundedness suffered is remembered in a person's spirit. As the child grows they will interpret each area of their life according to what they have already perceived life to be.

6. A baby growing inside the womb is just like the rest of us, and can experience a whole range of _____ even before entering this world. Some of these experiences may include:

   a. Failed Abortion - post-traumatic stress disorder; nightmares that might be in utero memories are:
      - "...it seems that most of the time they are about loved ones getting hurt or killed.."
      - "...If you think about it all my dreams have a recurring theme of saving myself which involves a lot of aggression, running, violence, getting help, defending myself and overcoming obstacles..."
      - "...I often dream about people dying, and in my dreams everyone else is nonchalant about it, yet I am terribly upset and wake up this way..."

- "...I have dreamed about being stabbed with a knife more than once..."
- "...I dream I am drowning..."

b. Siblings of an abortion and/or miscarriage may experience loss or trauma.

c. Adoption - Adults who have been adopted may experience emotions such as anxiety, rejection, or abandonment. Other symptoms of a child given up for adoption may be:

- Death wish and performance orientation
- Feelings of not belonging, being a burden, loneliness
- Fear of rejection may cause the child to need too much love or reject love altogether
- Pathological lying can occur due to the child being lied to either in the womb or during the formative years
- Kleptomania – the unborn judges that what was rightfully theirs was stolen from them
- Identity crisis may occur and exhibit fruit of trying to be everything to everyone because they fear rejection
- Resentment, defensiveness, anger, rebellion

d. If you experienced famine in utero, you are more prone as an adult to experience severe problems with being _____.

e. Confusion about your _____ _____.
Outwardly you may express your sex/gender but inwardly you may feel confused.
- The child that is identified as an "it" in the womb may feel like an "it" outside the womb.

- The child in the womb who knows that mom or dad wanted a child of the opposite sex experiences rejection and abandonment even before birth. As adults they may experience confusion concerning their sexual orientation.

7. In the 1960s scientists discovered a post-birth system of communication between the mother and child called _____.

   a. The womb environment has the ability to disrupt the formation of any stable _____ which can carry over into adolescence and adulthood, making trust and intimacy difficult to obtain.

   b. Researchers discovered the most important factor in the unborn child's development is the mother's _____ consistency.
      - One of the more harmful circumstances for an unborn child is when the _____ is absent, abusive or neglectful. An equally vital factor in the prenatal child's wellbeing is the father's commitment to the marriage.
      - If a mother experiences a significant _____ in her life that causes major distractions, she may withdraw her love and support from her unborn child. This loss may plunge the child into depression.

8. A _____ birth can contribute to traumatic experiences that may lead to emotional or spiritual issues in later life. Some studies are revealing that fibromyalgia and the chronic fatigue syndrome have their origins in severe traumatic births.

9. The attitudes and behavior of a person who is _____ in utero can be summed up in the message found in Psalm 109:22 stating *I'm so broken, needy and hurting. My heart is pierced through and I'm so wounded."* If you have been deeply wounded in utero, you will express that woundedness as child, adolescent, and adult.

Job 32:8 (Amplified Bible) *"But there is (a vital force) a spirit (of intelligence) in man, and the breath of the Almighty gives men understanding."* The woundedness you suffered is remembered in your spirit from your subconscious memories. Praise God - those memories can be healed through transformational healing prayer.

In utero Healing Prayer Testimony of former prison inmate Lisa Pedersen, age 25

When I went back to my mother's womb during the in utero healing, I remember being filled with anxiety and fear. I almost felt suffocated and closed in. I could feel my body tense up and I was almost in a fetal position in my chair. I had a hard time even breathing. After I was born, I felt such a physical and emotional release because I could rest in Jesus and knew I was going to be okay. Although my head was still pounding a bit, I could now breathe and sit up in my chair.

I learned from this in utero teaching the impact of my twin sister and my traumatic births on our lives. We were born 8 weeks prematurely and were kept at the hospital for two months. When we came home, we were kept on heart monitors. I was born naturally and my sister was breach so they took her by C-section.

Growing up both of us felt like we "struggled" through life and we had to fight for ourselves although school came a little easier for me. I always felt like a "bad" child growing up. I remember writing letters at an early age (7-8 years) to God expressing that I was not good and I caused my mom so much stress. Now I understand through this teaching that my mom's rough pregnancy and traumatic delivery was why I felt that way. In my teens,

I recognize now that I had a death wish – I would take stupid risks and make poor choices (including drug addiction) and I could never explain these things until now.

Through this in utero healing process, I understood and received the love my parents had for me. I could sense God's presence and I knew we were going to be okay. After the healing prayer with Patti and the ladies, they prayed over me and I broke the cycle of overwhelming anxiety that was passed down to me by my mom. And, the anxiety has truly been lifted off of me and I haven't experience a panic attack again. It was a great experience and very powerful. With God, I was healed when I replaced my lies with His Truth and unfailing presence and love. God has always been there with me and now I am open to receive His love.

PATTERNS AS RELATED TO IN-UTERO CONDITIONS

THE CONDITION IN-UTERO	COMMONLY OBSERVED PATTERNS OF ATTITUDE AND BEHAVIOR AFTER BIRTH
A child not wanted	Striving, performance orientation, trying to earn the right to be, inordinate desire to please (or the opposite, rejecting before they are rejected), tension, apologizing, anger, wishing death, frequent illness, problems with bonding, refusing affection (or having insatiable desire for same), never feels heard
A child conceived out of wedlock	Having a deep sense of shame, lack of belonging, feels different than others, lack of identity, struggles with relationship with Christ
The parents face a bad time financially	Believing "I am a burden," never asks for anything, becomes a financial miser
The parents are too young, not ready, bad timing	Believing "I am an intrusion," feels rejected, confused and feels like they live in the wrong time of life
The mother has poor health	Guilt for being: child may take emotional responsibility for mother

THE CONDITION IN-UTERO	COMMONLY OBSERVED PATTERNS OF ATTITUDE AND BEHAVIOR AFTER BIRTH
Rough pregnancy	Rejected, ignored, responsible for any pain mother experiences, expresses they feel they are "bad"
A child in utero being what one or both parents consider to be the wrong sex	Death wish. Sexual identification problems, sometimes one of the causes of homosexuality; striving to please to be what parents' want, futility, having a defeatist attitude: *"I was wrong from the beginning," "No matter what I do it will be wrong"* Rebellion-Why should I even try.
The child follows other conceptions that were lost	Being over-serious, over achieving, striving, trying to make up for the loss, anger at being a "replacement," not getting to be "me," struggles leaving home
Mother has a fear of delivery	Fear, insecurity, fear of birth; may choose in the womb not to be born, fear of doctors and hospitals
Fighting in the home	Nervous, fear, jumpiness, anxiety, panic attacks, parental inversion, responsible for others emotions, fear of being born, choosing never to grow up.
Father dies or leaves, father in service, prison, or works away from home more than being at home	Guilt, self-blame, bitter root expectation to be abandoned, inordinate hunger to find things to fill inner void, having a death wish, depression, anxiety, trouble bonding to men
Mother loses a loved one and is consumed with grief	Deep sadness, depression, having a death wish, fear of death, loneliness, imagining *"no support for me; I will have to depend on myself"*
Father unfaithful	Lack of trust toward men, lack of bonding toward men, vow to never become a man, bitter roots toward men
Unwholesome sexual relationship between father and mother	Aversion to sex, fear of male organ, sexual addictions, inability to climax or have intercourse

THE CONDITION IN-UTERO	COMMONLY OBSERVED PATTERNS OF ATTITUDE AND BEHAVIOR AFTER BIRTH
Toxemia	Fear of water, suffocating, at times feels like they are drowning
Mother does not eat properly	Fear of starving, food addictions, anger
Mother does not recognize pregnancy	Rejection, abandonment, believes they are invisible
Mother a heavy smoker	Predisposition to severe anxiety, fear of suffocating
Mother consumes much caffeine	Baby likely to have poor muscle tone and low activity level
Father physically abusive	Hatred toward men, fear of men, anxiety, takes responsibility they are the cause of abusive situations and they are "bad"
Child conceived through artificial insemination into a women who will carry the child but will not continue to mother the child after birth	Rejection, confusion, identity crisis, inability to trust or to bond
One parent practices homosexuality	Hatred toward sexuality, confusion of gender, protective of other parent, guilt, shame, inability to bond, doesn't want to be noticed

Testimony of Sharon Young, prison inmate for 32 years

When I heard the teaching on In Utero Trauma, I admit I was a bit skeptical about going back into the womb. It sounded kind of strange but I figured I trusted these women—if anything went wrong, they could pray me out of it.

I closed my eyes and said, "I'm open Lord if this is something you want for me." I was led to go back to my mother's womb and I did! I thought—I've done snapped because I became a fat little baby just swimming in my mother's womb. I felt everything.

I know that my parents didn't care and they thought I was stupid. I heard those lies even in the womb. They didn't want me. But it's okay that they didn't want me because I felt safe the womb. I innately knew Jesus loved me because He was there in the womb with me.

When I was ready to be born, I saw a little hole like a pencil end. I swam out. I wanted to be born! I was full of joy because Jesus loves me. I was safe in Him! I said "let's go – let's play!" I cried tears of joy. I saw the light and I was born into Jesus' arms. He really loves me! It was the most profound experience I have ever had.

Two weeks prior to this transformational healing prayer experience, I had a dream that I was holding a fat little baby. I was looking down at this baby. Initially, I didn't know if I was blessing this baby or telling it good-bye or what? Then I realized that I was crying tears of joy. I told my sister about my dream and told her that I had no idea who that baby was or why I was holding it. Very strange. When I went through the In Utero healing prayer, I realized that I was holding myself in that dream. Because I recognized that I was that same fat little baby from my dream two weeks earlier. **I actually felt God's love for the first time in my life.**

This is NOT the first time I felt God's love. However, I NEVER knew He loved me **even** then. Even **before** I was born. For the first time I knew He loved me from the womb.

Example of Healing Prayer

We are going to pray from Psalms 139:23-24 TPT. Say outloud after me: "God, I invite/ your searching gaze/ into my heart./ Examine me/ through and through/; find out everything/ that may be hidden/ within me./ Put me to the test /and sift through/ all my anxious cares./ See if there/ is any path of pain/ I'm walking on,/ and lead me back/ to your glorious, /everlasting ways—/ the path that brings me /back to You."

Hebrews 13: 8 *"Jesus Christ is the same yesterday, today and forever."*

Now, we're going to invite Holy Spirit to bring you back into your mother's womb:

1. **Seeker:** *Holy Spirit, I invite You to bring me back to my mother's womb. I trust You in this healing process to reveal to me what happened there.*

2. Tell us when you are there.

3. What do you see/sense?
   How do you feel?
   What pain is there?
   Are you ready to give that pain to Jesus?

   _____

   _____

   _____

   Seeker: *I give all this pain* _____ (put in hands and lift up to Jesus. Flip hands over when you feel you have given it all to Him) *to you Jesus. I choose by an act of my will to forgive my mom and dad for the pain they caused me.* Ask Jesus, what He will give you in exchange. Say: *Jesus, thank you for receiving all my pain. What will You give me in exchange for that pain?*

4. What emotions do you feel from your parents? **Seeker ask:** *Holy Spirit, please reveal to me what emotions I felt from my parents when I was in my mother's womb that have wounded me.*

   _____

   _____

   _____

In Jesus Christ's name, I break the power of ___(emotions)___ which I experienced in the womb. I cancel the assignment of those feelings/words. I forgive my mother/father and release them to you Jesus to have your perfect will and way in their lives. I declare all that has been taken by the enemy be restored to me in the name and blood of Jesus Christ.

Father, in the name of the Lord Jesus Christ, I speak to the inner spirit of _____ that her life is not a mistake. You have called this child into being at the right time and the right place. You have known this child from the very beginning. Father, You have never left nor forsaken this child.

5. **Seeker ask:** *Holy Spirit, please reveal to me what lies I believed in the womb.*

_____

_____

_____

Holy Spirit, what is Your Truth for me to counter/break that lie?

_____

_____

_____

Breaking Lies (Inner Vows/BRJ) Prayer

In the name of Jesus Christ I confess that I have believed the lie that _____ (lie) .

I make the choice to forgive _____ (name) *who caused me to believe this lie. I ask you, Jesus, to forgive me for believing this lie. I break the power of this lie that* _____ (lie) *in the name of Jesus Christ and I sever it with the Sword of the Spirit. What is the Truth from Your Word in exchange for that lie?* _____

I turn my back on this lie and choose to believe _____ (the Truth from God's Word) *and I can walk that out in Jesus Christ.*

6. <If Lack Father/Mother Love:> Father in the name of Jesus Christ Your word said that You are the Father and Mother to the orphans. This child of Yours is void of the love of the Father (Mother). I ask the Holy Spirit to come and fill the void of the Father's (Mother's) love. Fill _____'s centeredness that has been empty with Your perfect love.

7. **Seeker ask:** *Holy Spirit, show me if I am suffering from any physical disease due to in utero trauma?*

_____

_____

_____

Physical Healing Prayer

In Jesus Christ's name, I command complete healing and restoration over my body, soul, and spirit and specifically the healing of _____(disease)_____ *caused by in utero trauma. By Your stripes I am healed. Thank you Jesus.*

If needed, Break Generational Curses. Seeker ask:
Jesus are there any generational curses that I need to break today?

In the Name of Jesus Christ, I identify the sin pattern of_____ (name one at a time)_____. I forgive the past generations for walking in this particular sin and for bringing judgment/pain on me (and my family). I seek forgiveness for all the way(s) I have walked in the sin pattern. <I forgive _____(name)_____ my abuser> I break the power of the generational curse of ____(name sin)_____ in the Name and by the Blood of Jesus Christ and I place the cross of Jesus Christ between the curse and myself*. I make the choice to walk away from that sin and walk in obedience†. Amen

Add if applies: *I also forgive _____(name)_____ who abused me in this area.*

* *Placing the cross in prayer between you and an area of sin is a type of symbolic or visual prayer. If the cross is between you and the sin, then you have to go back through the cross to pick the sin up again.*

† *This may mean not to drink alcohol, buy pornographic materials, or whatever else the sin may be.*

8. Are you ready to be born into the arms of Jesus?
   Seeker: *Jesus, I know that You knit me together in my mother's womb. That You are the same yesterday, today and forever. So, I invite you to hold me as I am born. I am ready...*

9. Can you describe what is happening?
   What is Jesus doing?
   What is He saying to you?
   How are you feeling?

10. Blessing Prayer*: I pray that the eyes of your heart, _____(seeker)_____, may be enlightened so that you may know the hope of His calling, the riches of the glory of His inheritance in the saints, and the surpassing greatness of His power toward you. May God grant you, _____(seeker)_____, according to His riches and glory, to be strengthened with power through His Holy Spirit in the inner man. We seal all these prayers with oil in the name of the Father, Son, and Holy Spirit. Amen.

* Additional Father and Mother Blessing Prayers on pages 33-38.

In Utero Healing Prayer Testimony of inmate Heather Speakman, age 34

I sat in a chair closing my eyes taking myself back to the moments in my mother's womb. Feelings of rejection, abandonment, and a very dark sadness was all around me. I didn't want to come out. I wanted to stay in the dark. Patti asked me if I sensed Jesus was there? I didn't at first but then it started getting brighter and brighter. I had an overwhelming feeling that I need to get to that Light. I needed to get out. I wanted to be born. I felt purpose in my life for the first time. I felt love.

My In Utero healing has revealed many deep wounds that I continue to take Jesus with me to get to the root of it. I am truly blessed to have been taught this teaching. My life is forever changed and I will share this teaching with my family.

Suggested Reading Material for Further Studies:

The Secret Life of the Unborn Child,
Thomas Verny

Healing the Wounded Spirit, John and Paula Sandford

Restoring the Christian Soul, Leanne Payne

 ## Breakthrough Declarations

1. I am fearfully and wonderfully made (Psalm 139:14).

2. I am God's workmanship, created in Christ Jesus to do good works, which God has prepared in advance for me to do (Ephesians 2:10).

3. I am a man/woman created in God's image (Genesis 1:27).

4. All that has been stolen from me will be redeemed for His glory (Isaiah 59:15-16; Colossians 1:13).

5. Through Jesus I am 100% loved and worthy to receive all of God's blessings (Galatians 3:1-5).

* Some declarations used with permission of Steve and Wendy Backlund with IgnitingHope.com

1. mind
   personality
2. world
   soul
3. significant
4. conception
5. womb
6. emotions
   d. overweight
   e. sexual orientation
7. bonding
   a. attachment
   b. emotional
   - father
   - loss
8. traumatic
9. wounded

Father Forgiveness Blessing Prayer

May I have your permission to speak to you as your father?

Let these be like the words that your father would have spoken to you, if he could have separated from his wounds and if he could have received the love and mercy of the true Father and had His heart to share with you. Let it help release your father from any bitterness you may have toward him and restore a true image into your heart of what your Heavenly Father is really like.

I ask your forgiveness for the things that I have done that have hurt you... Please forgive me... for failing to accept and affirm you
- For not showing you respect for your uniqueness.
- For not giving you freedom to form and express your own opinions.
- For not making you feel that you were the boy/girl I wanted.
- For not giving you the affection and acceptance you needed.
- For not telling you "I love you" and hugging you regularly.
- Will you forgive me?

Please forgive me... for neglecting my responsibilities
- For not keeping my word or my promises to you.
- For not apologizing to you and admitting when I was wrong.
- For not protecting you and making you feel safe.
- For not providing for you financially.
Will you forgive me?

Please forgive me... for abandoning you
- For not giving you my time and attention.
- For not being at your sports games and special events.
- For my silence toward you.
- For abandoning you emotionally and physically.
- For not quitting my addictions for your sake.

Will you forgive me?

Please forgive me... for verbal and physical abuse
- For not building you up, encouraging you and believing in you.
- For embarrassing you in front of others.
- For yelling at you and cursing you in my anger.
- For disciplining you with harshness—making you fear me.
- For physically or sexually abusing you.

Will you forgive me?

Please forgive me... for failing as a husband to your mother
- For not loving your mother.
- For not showing you a man's true responsibilities in the home.
- For not marrying your mother before you were conceived.
- For the times of physical and verbal abuse of her you saw and heard.
- For divorcing your mom and abandoning you.
- Can you forgive me for dying?

Will you forgive me?

Please forgive me... for being a poor spiritual leader; poor role model
- For not being a godly father, for not praying for you or with you.
- For not taking you to church and teaching you about the Lord.
- For not taking a stand for what is right.
- For not modeling for you a healthy picture of the true Father.

Will you forgive me?

I ask your forgiveness for all the ways I was not there for you when you needed me.

I'd like to walk you through this PRAYER TO FORGIVE YOUR FATHER if you are willing. I will give you time to repeat this prayer out loud after me.

Dear Heavenly Father,/ in the name of Jesus,/ I purpose and choose/ by an act of my will/ to forgive my father/ for all the ways that he failed me/ or hurt me./ I repent for agreeing with the enemy/ in bitterness about my father./ I renounce those things in my life./ Now, in the name of Jesus/ I recieve Your forgiveness of me/ and I choose to forgive myself/ and to fully accept myself/ as the child of the father You gave me./

Holy Spirit please come.../ heal my broken heart/ and show me and tell me your truth...

Now I want to give you your FATHER'S BLESSING

Please receive this as if these were the words your father would speak to you if he could be free to receive the heavenly Father's love for you.

- I bless you my precious child. You are so loved—specially created by God, unique and perfect. I am so proud of you. I speak life into you.
- I bless all the relationships of your life that you may grow in friendship and intimacy with your Heavenly Father, with your Lord and Savior Jesus Christ, with the Holy Spirit, and with all your friends and family members.
- I bless your ability to be strong in the Lord and in the power of His might, that you may be a mighty spiritual warrior serving the purposes of God in your generation.
- I bless you and release you into the gifts God has given you to fulfill His plan for you. I love you.

Used with permission of Reverend Annie Arakelian, Clinical Christian Counselor and Board Certified Life Coach. http://lightofthecomforter.org/prayer-for-forgivenesshealingblessing_father-child/

Mother Forgiveness Blessing Prayer

May I have your permission to speak to you as your mother?

Let these be like the words that your mother would have spoken to you, if she could have separated from her wounds and if she could have received the love and mercy of the true Father and had His heart to share with you. Let it help you release your mother from any bitterness you may have toward her and restore a true image into your heart of what your Heavenly Father is really like.

I ask your forgiveness for the things that I have done that have hurt you...
Please forgive me... for failing to accept and affirm you
- For not telling you how precious you were to me.
- For not making you feel that you were the boy/girl I wanted.
- For not giving you the affection and acceptance you needed.
- For giving you up for adoption or for conceiving you out of wedlock.
- It's not your fault. You were not a mistake.
Will you forgive me?

Please forgive me... for poor parenting
- For not letting you enjoy being a child.
- For not protecting you from all the fussing and fighting in our home.
- For not believing you or protecting you from your father's abuse.
- For telling you it was your fault. It was not your fault.
Will you forgive me?

Please forgive me... for taking my emotions out on you
- For telling you that you'd never amount to anything.
- For the anger and frustration I took out on you.
- For saying words that devalued you and shamed you.
- For not giving you freedom to form and express your own opinions.
Will you forgive me?

Please forgive me... for failing to nurture you
- For not showing you unconditional love.
- For not holding you when you were hurt.
- For not taking the time to meet your needs.
- For not spending time with you because I was always busy.
- For not quitting my addictions for your sake.

Will you forgive me?

Please forgive me... for smothering you
- For controlling you and making you do things my way.
- For getting angry if you tried to express your independence.
- For trying to control your every action.
- For manipulating you with guilt and threatened rejection.

Will you forgive me?

Please forgive me... for not being a godly role model
- For not modeling what a godly wife and mother should be.
- For not taking you to church or teaching you to pray.
- For divorcing your father.
- Can you forgive me for dying?

Will you forgive me?

I ask your forgiveness for all the ways I was not there for you when you needed me.

Prayer to Forgive Your Mother (for the Child)*
Client Say: *Dear Heavenly Father,/ in the name of Jesus/ I purpose and choose/ by an act of my will/ to forgive my mother/ for all the ways she failed me/ or hurt me./ I repent for agreeing with the enemy/ in bitterness about my mother./ I renounce those things in my life./ Now, in the name of Jesus,/ I receive Your forgiveness of me/ and I choose to forgive myself/ and to fully accept myself/ as the child of the mother You gave me./ Holy Spirit please come.../ heal my broken heart/ and show me and tell me your truth...*

Mother's Blessing

Please receive this as if these were the words your mother would speak to you if she could be free to receive the heavenly Father's love for you.

- I bless you my precious child. You are so loved—specially created by God, unique and perfect. I am so proud of you. I speak life into you.
- I bless your heart that your spouse, friends and children can safely trust in it, that you will have a grateful heart and be thankful for all you have been given.
- I bless your fear of the Lord, that you may follow His commandments, walk in His ways and desire to have order and balance in your life.
- Before you were born God loved you and I love you. I honor you. I praise God for you. I bless you now and forever.

Used with permission of Reverend Annie Arakelian, Clinical Christian Counselor and Board Certified Life Coach From: http://thelightofthecomforter. com/2016/prayer-for-forgivenesshealingblessing_mother-child/

_____

_____

_____

_____

_____

_____

_____

_____

_____

_____

_____

_____

_____

_____

_____

_____

_____

Who Owns This Problem?

I ran an errand for my husband Jim at a discount equipment supply company. It was a long drive and he had called in advance to ensure that the item he wanted me to pick up was at the store. I was on my way home from a speaking engagement so I was all dressed up in a suit and heels feeling very out of place at this store which was clearly for men.

Jim had texted me the item number only, not the name of the item as he had promised. The on-line item numbers were several digits longer than the numbers he had texted me. When the store clerk finally figured out what he wanted, they had none in stock. I called Jim up to clarify. He yelled at me because of the store's incompetence. After the young man finished helping me, he said to me "You should never let anyone treat you that way!" I shrugged my shoulders and said "What can I do?" He replied, "That's what your hand is for. You should backhand him and tell him he shouldn't treat you that way." I sighed and said,

"This week it will be 31 years we've been married." He looked at me with such pity in his eyes and stated, "That's a really long time..." and he walked away.

As I was driving home, I wanted to say to that young man—Jim wasn't always like that. When I married him he was a strong Christian who had daily devotions and loved God. He served as a deacon in our first church.

I sadly recalled our conversation less than a week previous when Jim admitted that although he still believed in God, he didn't believe that God cared about him or had a plan for his life. He had no interest in attending church or pursuing a relationship with God because God ignored him when he prayed so why bother?

For too long, I tried to change so that he wouldn't verbally abuse me. Ask fewer questions about why or how something worked. Avoid ever questioning one of his decisions. Do more for him (put his clothes away, pick up after him). Do everything around the house that I could. Have very few expectations of him. Earn more money so there wouldn't be financial strain. Don't give suggestions for how something might work better. Always forgive him after he yelled at me (he usually said he was sorry but then failed to change his behavior), give that pain to Jesus to carry for me. I tried very hard to not be offended by his yelling and always believe the best about him.

At least moving to the country and 5 acres there was less chance that neighbors would hear him. Our oldest son Bryan moved back in with us for his last two years of college and I realized we had reversed roles. It used to be that I protected Bryan from Jim's yelling at him. Now Bryan began to protect me from his yelling.

So this must be what it is like to live with an abuser. It happens so slowly that it is like the frog in the boiling water. You don't really know that you are being boiled because the temperature heats up so slowly that you don't recognize it. I felt trapped. Alone. Depressed. It was like living with the enemy every day. I was stunned. How could I—a very talented and highly accom-

plished professional speaker and author feel self-rejection, yet just recently I had begun to feel that way. For years, I doubted myself as a wife because of how Jim treated me. Now I was beginning to transfer that to my professional life. I no longer felt effective. My client feedback was still positive but I had begun to doubt myself.

The lies of the enemy taunted me. I knew I had to deal with myself... but also deal with Jim's verbal abuse. I could no longer own Jim's verbal abuse as being my problem nor could I be his Holy Spirit. I needed to own my problems and let Jim own his anger issues.

Shortly thereafter, I separated from Jim and left our home for nine months. I gave Jim four things he must deal with before I would consider staying married as none of those things were my problem.

Only until Jim owned his problems and I owned mine and we went through an intensive counseling process for a year and a half were we reconciled only by the grace of God. We each needed to experience healing in our souls before we could work on our marriage. Problem ownership and establishing healthy boundaries is key in any relationship.

Your job is to own your own problems and not own other people's problems. Too often we focus on helping or controlling other people so that we don't have to confront our own issues. Identifying one's own problems leads to the healing of root issues in your life.

1. What is "Problem Ownership"?

> **"Bear each other's burdens (Greek "baros"), and in this way you will fulfill the law of Christ. If anyone thinks he is something when he is nothing, he deceives himself. Each one should test his actions. Then he can take pride in himself, without comparing himself to somebody else, for each one should carry his own load (Greek "phortion")."**
> **Galatians 6:2-5** (New International Version)

a. "Baros" defined: _____, trouble. When someone is carrying a heavy burden that is pressing down, they need help to carry it.

b. "Phortion" defined: a _____. Each person must bear their own load because only they can bear it.

2. Challenges to not understanding healthy problem ownership:

   a. Many Christians are out to rescue the world and are more in touch with others' problems than they are with their _____ problems.

   b. Rescuing and owning other's problems can become _____ and can become a way of _____ your self.

   c. When you incorrectly carry other's burdens, you are subject to _____ because you are carrying problems that are not your own.

3. If you take the problems of others and handle them, then you are treating that person as a _____. This does not give them the opportunity to grow up. You may come across as controlling. Eventually the person who owns the problem will resent you and not want you to interfere in their life.

Which of these challenges do you struggle most with?

_____

_____

_____

_____

4. In all the problems of life, one must decide ***who really
_____ the problem***.

- **I own it:**
  If I own the problem, _____ must take action to solve the problem.
- **You own it:**
  If you own the problem,_____ must take action to solve the problem.
- **We own it:**
  If we own the problem, _____ must take action to solve the problem.
- **Nobody owns it:**
  If no one owns the problem, _____ solution is necessary.

Adapted from Gail Eillis of Lakewood Presbyterian Church in Lakewood, Ohio, has put together the following helpful checklists:

WHEN I FEEL RESPONSIBLE *for* OTHERS, I...
- fix
- protect
- rescue
- control
- carry their feelings
- don't listen

WHEN I FEEL RESPONSIBLE *to* OTHERS, I come alongside others by...
- showing empathy
- encouraging
- sharing
- confronting
- being sensitive
- listening

WHEN I FEEL RESPONSIBLE *for* OTHERS, I FEEL...
- tired
- anxious
- fearful
- liable

WHEN I FEEL RESPONSIBLE *to* OTHERS, I FEEL...
- relaxed
- free
- aware
- valued

WHEN I FEEL RESPONSIBLE *for* OTHERS, I am concerned with . . .

- the solution
- the answer
- circumstances
- being right
- details
- performance

WHEN I FEEL RESPONSIBLE *to* OTHERS, I am concerned with . . .

- relating person-to-person as equal to others
- listening to others feelings and thoughts
- respecting the person

Bottom Line:

- I am a manipulator
- I expect the person to live up to my expectations

Bottom Line:

- I am a helper/guide
- I can trust and let go

5. Five reasons why you get caught up in unhealthy problem ownership:

   a. Unhealed _____ issues. The past is not the past until you deal with it.

   b. Poor _____-_____.

   c. _____ beliefs (inner vows, Bitter Root Judgments, etc.)

   d. _____ characteristics. Enabling behavior.

   e. Misconceptions of what is _____.

   Which of these reasons cause you to get caught up in unhealthy relationships?

   _____

   _____

   _____

   _____

   _____

   _____

Jan Gossner, a theologian from Oslo, Norway has developed a survey that will help you look at yourself.

RESPONSIBILITY CHECKLIST

(Place the number that best describes your answer in the space provided.)

Total lack of Responsibility 1	Under Responsible 2	Peaceful, Relaxed, Responsible 3	Over Responsible 4	Hyper Responsible 5

1. As a child, I was _____.

2. Mother would say I was _____.

3. Dad would say I was _____.

4. My spouse, roommate or close friend would say I was _____.

5. I say I am at _____ today.

6. I want to be _____ as soon as possible.

Remember it is easy to become out of balance if you **react fast** and **think later**.

6. Correct/healthy problem ownership means:

   a. I'm responsible for my _____.
      I'm not responsible for others _____.

   b. I'm responsible for my _____.
      I'm not responsible for others _____.

   c. I'm responsible for my _____.
      I'm not responsible for others _____.

   d. I'm responsible for my _____.
      I'm not responsible for others _____.

---

e. I'm responsible for _____, and I only have the _____ to change me.

f. I'm not responsible for _____, nor do I have the _____ to change anything about you!

In what relationships do you most struggle with problem ownership?

_____
_____
_____
_____
_____
_____
_____
_____
_____
_____
_____

"In everything, therefore, treat people the same way you want them to treat you."

Matthew 7:12 (NASV)

7. Using the acronym B.E.A.R., we can look at what scripture has to say about problem ownership:

B = _____ – to stand beside and "bear watching" another handle their own pain.

E = _____ – to love someone unconditionally as they struggle *through* their problems. *"You seem to be _____, are you?"*

A = _____ – to let go. Don't assume a person wants you to do something just because they are sharing with you.

R = _____ – to walk beside the person and intercede for them.

8. Five steps to identify who owns the problem(s):

   1. _____. Many times you may be thinking of a response to make in conversation instead of really listening to the person who is talking. It is OK if there is silence in the conversation.

   "My dear brothers, take note of this: Everyone should be quick to listen, slow to speak and slow to become angry."

   James 1:19 (NIV)

   2. _____ what is the real problem. Pretend that you are watching the event but the sound is on mute. You see the event but you cannot hear the event.
      a. *What are you seeing?* Then think about the emotions behind the words.
      b. *What do you believe about what you have heard?* Is your belief Biblically based? If not, what needs to be changed.

   3. _____ the situation by asking good questions. This discussion will help identify if you, the other person, or both of you own the problem. Perhaps no one owns the problem.

   4. _____. When you are not sure, take time out. Take the situation to God in prayer. Pray in the Spirit if you don't know how to pray for the situation.

> *"In the same way, the Spirit helps us in our weakness. We do not know what we ought to pray for, but the Spirit Himself intercedes for us with groans that words cannot express. And He who searches our hearts knows the mind of the Spirit, because the Spirit intercedes for the saints in accordance with God's will."*
>
> **Romans 8:26-27** (NIV)

5. _____ and _____.
   If the problem is the other person's, affirm their ability to handle the situation. Pray for them and with them.

A goal in life should be to move toward peaceful, relaxed, and responsible relationships. When we trust in God we are able to let go of the issues that others need to deal with. A good rule of thumb is to ask yourself the question, ***"Will this issue make a difference with the eternal life of the person?"*** If the answer is "no", then perhaps the issue needs to be put into proper perspective.

You cannot own another's pain or unhealthy beliefs. You must point them to Jesus who has the healing and answers.

Exercises in Problem Ownership

Look over the examples to decide (a) what is the problem, and (b) who owns the problem.

1. Maria had an important appointment at 3:30 p.m. She goes out to start the car and it won't start. Maria becomes upset with her husband because husbands are to protect their wives by keeping their cars running smoothly.

    Problem _____

    Who owns it? _____

2. Jose and Ruth are having marriage problems. Ruth comes over and in tears asks you whether or not she should get a divorce.

    Problem _____

    Who owns it? _____

3. Willie has promised to take his family to a movie. The phone rings and on the other end is John, who is crying and obviously drunk. Willie knows that John is an alcoholic. Willie has ministered to John many times before and has continued to pray for him, but John's been unwilling to face the truth. Willie told John not to call when he's been drinking.

    Problem _____

    Who owns it? _____

4. Diamond is responsible for all bill writing and keeping tabs on the checkbook. Henry, her husband, uses the "Anytime Bank" for withdrawals and neglects to tell Diamond. Their car payment is returned in the mail for lack of funds.

   Problem _____

   Who owns it? _____

5. Tyrone and Todd are roommates. At the beginning of the relationship it was agreed that Todd would clean and Tyrone would cook. Tyrone has kept his end of the agreement, but Todd hasn't cleaned since they moved in several months ago.

   Problem _____

   Who owns it? _____

6. Asia and Jane are your two best friends. Recently Asia lent Jane some money and expected to be paid back within a week. Jane has not paid Asia back, and she is angry at Jane because she needs the money to pay her car insurance. Asia has asked you to talk to Jane for her.

   Problem _____

   Who owns it? _____

7. Judy has become a very critical person concerning church. It seems like every time you get together, she criticizes the church leaders.

   Problem _____

   Who owns it? _____

Breakthrough Declarations

1. I care about others and therefore allow them sto own their own problems. (Proverbs 19:19).

2. I trust in God and am able to let go of the issues that others need to deal with (Romans 8:26-27).

3. I listen before I speak and ask good questions (James 1:19).

4. I have the wisdom of God today. I will think the right thoughts, say the right words, and make the right decisions in every situation I face (James 1:5; 1 Corinthians 2:16).

5. I trust that God has my children's best interests in mind and He will lead, guide, and direct them (Isaiah 40:11; Jeremiah 29:11).

* Some declarations used with permission of Steve and Wendy Backlund with IgnitingHope.com

Think about a situation involving **conflict** that you either observed or were involved in this week. **Describe** the situation and **identify** problem ownership.

_____

_____

_____

_____

_____

_____

_____

_____

_____

_____

_____

_____

_____

Recommended Reading

I Don't Have to Make Everything All Better by Gary and Joy Lundberg, Penguin Books, 2000.

1. a. burden   b. load
2. a. own   b. addictive avoiding   c. burnout
3. child
4. owns
   I
   You
   We
   No
5. a. past
   b. self-image
   c. ungodly
   d. codependent
   e. truth
6. a. emotions   emotions
   b. thoughts   thoughts
   c. beliefs   beliefs
   d. actions   actions
   e. me   ability
   f. you   ability
7. Bear   Empathy   Action   Respect
8. (1) Listen
   (2) Identify
   (3) Clarify
   (4) Delay
   (5) Affirm and Empower

Exercise answers
1. Maria
2. Ruth
3. Willie
4. both
5. Tyrone
6. Asia
7. Judy

Breaking Your Inner Vows

When you're six feet tall as a girl in high school you better do something with that height. I did play basketball but not all tall girls do play basketball. I also was in track and field but basketball was my main sport.

My main goal in playing basketball was to earn the Most Valuable Player award... because I was the "most valuable player" of my team. I played varsity basketball for three years. I was consistently the highest scorer. I still hold the record for most points scored in a single game. I usually had the most rebounds as that's how I got my points. By all statistical measures, I should have been the MVP.

My junior year, I was ready... but they named a senior girl the MVP. By my senior year I knew it was my year... but, the girls on my team selected a junior for the award. I was angry. I couldn't believe it. Even the coaches were shocked so they created a special award for me that year—the "3 year award." I think that must be something like going to the Miss America pageant and getting named "Miss Congeniality"—nice but ugly!

I was devastated and I made an inner vow: I will never play competitive sports with girls again (and I didn't). And, I just don't fit in with girls my age. I never really had a "best friend" in high school. My best neighborhood friend moved away in the 7th grade and I never really found another. This MVP selection confirmed my beliefs.

Now that seems quite harmless, doesn't it? However my vow translated to: I didn't play college basketball but instead sought out leadership roles. I was a Resident Advisor for two years in college, and elected to student government. All good things right?

But here's the downside: After college and marriage, I didn't really get involved in women's events unless I was in charge because I didn't feel I had anything in common with them. I didn't have a group of women my own age that I would I really call friends for many years.

This inner vow prevented me from blessing me and caused me to make Bitter Root Judgments as well which we will cover in the next lesson...

It is easy to block yourself from God's blessings by unknowingly cursing/hurting yourself. This breakthrough lesson will teach you the importance of your own words and the impact they can have on your life. Enjoy the newfound freedom by breaking your inner vows and living more freely in Christ.

"For as he thinks in his heart so he is."
Proverbs 23:7 (AKJV)

1. The enemy of your soul wants nothing more than to prevent you from fulfilling your destiny by entangling you with _____.

2. Self-inflicted _____ come from your own belief system.

   a. Self-inflicted curses are made often at an early age from your own _____.

   b. Self-inflicted curses also come about by the choice not to _____ *and* not to _____ the truth, which is revealed to you in God's Word.

> *"The weapons of warfare are not carnal, but mighty through God to the pulling down of strongholds: Casting down imaginations and every high thing that exalts itself against the knowledge of God and bringing into captivity every thought to the obedience of Christ."*
>
> **2 Corinthians 10: 4-5 (KJV)**

3. Inner vows are your belief system about _____.

   a. These self-inflicted curses are expressed through your thoughts and words.

   b. Inner vows are made to _____ you from being wounded or hurt again. As a result, those vows significantly impact your relationships because that vow influences how you respond in different situations and to other people.

> *Keep your thoughts continually fixed on all that is authentic and real, honorable and admirable, beautiful and respectful, pure and holy, merciful and kind. And fasten your thoughts on every glorious work of God, praising him always.*
>
> **Philippians 4: 8** (TPT)

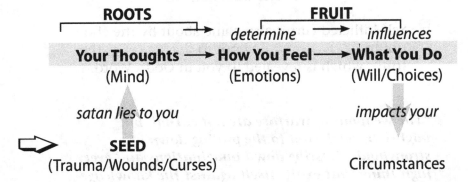

ROOTS   **FRUIT**

determine → *influences*

Your Thoughts → **How You Feel** → **What You Do**
(Mind)   (Emotions)   (Will/Choices)

satan lies to you   *impacts your*

SEED
(Trauma/Wounds/Curses)   Circumstances

> *Watch your words and be careful what you say, and you'll be surprised by how few troubles you'll have.*
>
> **Proverbs 21: 23** (TPT)
>
> *"The tongue has the power of life and death, and those who love it will eat its fruit."*
>
> **Proverbs 18: 21** (NIV)

4. Inner vows prevent you from blessing _____.
   Inner vows begin with the word "I" such as
   - **I** *will never love again.*
   - **I** *will never trust again.*
   - **I** *won't try again.*
   - **I** *hate myself.*
   - **I** *am stupid.*

a. Inner vows are often what hold the person in the cycle of old _____.

b. Inner vows resist normal _____.

> **"Again, you have heard that it was said to the people a long time ago, Do not break your oath, but keep the oaths you have made to the Lord." But I tell you, do not swear at all: either by heaven, for it is His footstool; or by Jerusalem, for it is the city of the Great King."**
>
> **Matthew 5: 33** (NIV)

5. The five characteristics of an inner vow

1) A distinctive mark of an inner vow is that it resists the normal _____ process in an individual. 1 Corinthians 13: 11 tells us *"When I was a child, I talked like a child, I reasoned like a child. When I became a man, I put childish ways behind me."*

    Example: Children raised in a home where adults were abusive may create an image within themselves that to become an adult means to become abusive.

 **Activation Exercise**

Physically stand up and give yourself permission to be a man or woman. Say out loud:

By an act of my will, I give myself permission to become a man/ woman. While I can still have fun and enjoy life, I choose to put childish ways behind me. I choose to be responsible. I choose to become the man/woman that God created me to be. Thank you for Holy Spirit's empowerment to change. Amen.

---

2) Vows that are made as an adult will _____ the person. Vows that are made as a child are _____ the person.

> *Numbers 30: 3-5* [The Message] *states "When a woman makes a vow to God and binds herself by a pledge as a young girl still living in her father's house, and her father hears of her vow or pledge but says nothing to her, then she has to make good on all her vows and pledges. But if her father holds her back when he hears of what she has done, none of her vows and pledges are valid. God will release her since her father held her back."*

 This is one of the reasons it is so important for parents to speak _____ into the lives of their children (or any child) whenever they hear an inner vow being expressed.

3) The affects of the child's vow become deeply _____ into the core belief system of the child. The inner vow becomes part of the foundation that the person builds their life choices upon.

 **When a person is saved through Jesus Christ, these vows remain as _____ _____ that interfere with the process of growing up in the character of Christ. The power of these vows *must* be broken. This battle is self-inflicted.**

---

4) When an inner vow is made as an adult, it creates conflict but does not become part of the foundation of the person's life. An inner vow made as an adult affects the person's _____ and _____.

   Example: Israel's complaining

5) Inner vows may not manifest immediately but often will lie dormant until a person or situation _____ them. Many different things can trigger inner vows that have been dormant. Healing is a continual process. Never assume everything has been taken care of.

If you overreact to a person or situation, it may be that your inner vow, that had laid dormant for years, was suddenly triggered. You may react to that trigger with the emotions of a child at the age when you were first wounded.

Our inner healing process can be compared to revealing the different layers in an onion – one layer at a time.

Pray and Ask: *Holy Spirit, please show me if there are any triggers or inner vows I've made that you want to heal with me?*

_____

_____

_____

_____

Examples of Common Inner Vows that lead to Unhealthy Patterns/Fruit:

- ❏ I am bad.
- ❏ I am ugly.
- ❏ I am stupid.
- ❏ I am dirty.
- ❏ I hate my body.
- ❏ I hate being a woman (or man).
- ❏ I never want children.
- ❏ I will never love again.
- ❏ I will never trust again.
- ❏ I will never allow myself to be vulnerable.
- ❏ I never want to get married (or remarried).
- ❏ I will never cry.
- ❏ I never want to grow up.
- ❏ My abilities aren't good enough.
- ❏ I will keep the secret.
- ❏ I will never tell anyone the truth about my family.
- ❏ I never want to be like my parent(s).
- ❏ I hate _____.
- ❏ I don't need your help.
- ❏ I cannot succeed.
- ❏ It always happens to me.
- ❏ I have to make you happy.
- ❏ I'll never meet God's standards.
- ❏ Why even try?
- ❏ This is what I deserve.
- ❏ I'll get even.
- ❏ I'll always be afraid.
- ❏ It's hopeless.
- ❏ I'll never change.
- ❏ I can't do it.
- ❏ My faith isn't strong enough.
- ❏ I'll always be lonely.
- ❏ I have nothing to offer.
- ❏ If people only knew…
- ❏ I'll never amount to anything.
- ❏ I'm not worthy.
- ❏ I'll never try again.
- ❏ I always disappoint myself.
- ❏ Every time I try, I fail.
- ❏ I don't fit in.
- ❏ I won't share my heart.
- ❏ I never get what I want.
- ❏ I can do it all by myself.
- ❏ Emotions are to be kept to yourself.
- ❏ I always get sick.

Some inner vows are very simple while others are very complex. Others may be hard to understand.

7. The process of breaking your inner vows

   a. Identify the event or person in your life that caused you to make the inner vow. Go back to the first time you recall thinking/speaking your inner vow. Ask Holy Spirit to help you recognize what it cost you and the pain you feel.

   b. Choose to forgive the person/people involved.

   c. Ask God to forgive yourself for believing that inner vow.

   d. Sever the inner vow with the Sword of the Spirit.

   e. Turn your back on your inner vow by choosing the Truth and walking in that Truth.

Ask Jesus: *Jesus, are ther any specific inner vows you want me to deal with?*

_____

_____

_____

_____

_____

_____

_____

_____

_____

_____

_____

Sample Healing Prayer

Inner Vow I want to deal with:

_____

_____

_____

Before we do the healing prayer, I want you to say: *Holy Spirit, please show me the pain that this inner vow has cost me in my life.*

_____

_____

_____

Holy Spirit, show me if I am suffering from any physical disease due to my inner vows?

_____

_____

_____

In the name of Jesus Christ I confess that I have believed the inner vow that _____(vow)_____. Jesus, I give you my inner vow of _____(vow)_____ and the pain it has caused me _____(pain)_____. Jesus, what is Your Truth in exchange for my inner vow? _____(His Truth)_____.
In Jesus Christ's name, I command complete healing and restoration of _____(disease)_____ caused by my inner vow. By Your stripes I am healed. Thank you Jesus. I make the choice to forgive
_____(name)_____ whose sin against me enabled me to make this inner vow. I ask you, Jesus, to forgive me for believing my inner vow. I break the power of this inner vow
_____(vow)_____ in the name of Jesus Christ and I sever it with the Sword of the Spirit. I renounce any demonization that exists as a result of my inner vow. Now I turn my back on this vow and choose instead to believe
_____(Truth)_____ and I can walk it out in the powerful name of Jesus Christ.

Breakthrough Declarations

1. I am the head, not the tail. I have insight. I have wisdom. I have ideas and divine strategies. I have authority (Deuteronomy 28:13, 8:18; James 1:5-8; Luke 10:19).

2. I expect the best day of my life spiritually, emotionally, relationally, and financially in Jesus' name (Romans 15:13).

3. I speak to the raging waters in my life; peace, be still. I say to my mind; peace, be still. I say to my emotions; peace, be still. I say to my body; peace, be still. I say to my home; peace, be still. I say to my family; peace, be still (Mark 4:39).

4. My prayers are powerful and effective (2 Corinthians 5:21; James 6:16b).

5. My angels are carrying out the Word of God on my behalf (Psalm 103:20).

* Declarations used with permission of Steve and Wendy Backlund with IgnitingHope.com

Fill-in-the-Blank Answer Guide

1. strongholds
2. curses
    a. woundedness
    b. believe, obey
3. yourself   protect
4. you
    a. patterns
    b. change
5. 1) maturing
    2) affect   set into   truth
    3) rooted   ungodly beliefs
    4) choices, habits
    5) trigger

Personal Victory Journal of Your Healing Progress

 You may want to make a list of the Inner Vows you have broken as well as the Truth as a reminder to you of your inner healing progress:

My Inner Vows: God's Truth:

_____   _____

_____   _____

_____   _____

_____   _____

_____   _____

_____   _____

_____   _____

_____   _____

_____   _____

_____   _____

_____   _____

_____   _____

_____   _____

_____   _____

_____   _____

_____   _____

_____   _____

_____   _____

_____   _____

Use additional pages if you need more room.

Gaining Freedom from Bitter Root Judgments

Let me tell you about Miss Leisman... She was my 5th grade teacher.

Up until 5th grade, I was a model for "teacher's pet" but that all changed with Miss Leisman. Miss Leisman was never married and she walked stiff as a board with her sister, also an unmarried teacher.

I loved my other teachers and would write cute notes on the top of my papers, like "I liked this assignment ☺." And my other elementary teachers wrote me sweet notes back or gave me extra approval stickers. Do you see my "need for performance" coming through here even as a child?

Well, Miss Leisman made it very clear that she did not appreciate nor liked my notes as they were childish and should not continue.

My sweet little, teacher's-pet personality turned evil and I made life for Miss Leisman a living hell for that year. I later learned that they had special meetings about my group of friends on how to deal with us.

I learned in this lesson and now understand that I had a Bitter Root Judgment against my teacher – "You are not going to tell me what I can and can't do" and a rebellious spirit entered me against authority figures that lasted into my adult life.

In the last lesson we covered Inner Vows, which prevents you from blessing you. Now you will learn how you prevent others from blessing you. Do you want to be blessed? You may not realize that it may be your own judgments that prevent others from blessing you. In this lesson you will learn how to release your Bitter Root Judgments which may change your personal relationships for the better.

> **"Each heart knows its own bitterness and no one else can share the joy."**
>
> **Proverbs 14: 10**
>
> **"See to it that no one misses the grace of God and that no bitter root grows up to cause trouble and defile many."**
>
> **Hebrews 12: 15** (NIV)

1. Bitter Root Judgments prevent _____ from blessing _____.

    a. Bitter Root Judgments are made as a result of painful events (or woundedness) in your life. The judgment actually gains strength, even to the point it may become a major _____ in your life.

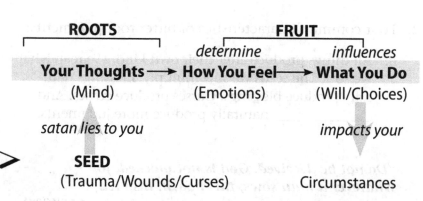

ROOTS | FRUIT

determine | *influences*

Your Thoughts ⟶ **How You Feel** ⟶ **What You Do**
(Mind) (Emotions) (Will/Choices)

satan lies to you *impacts your*

SEED Circumstances
(Trauma/Wounds/Curses)

b. Those judgments are like a wall of
_____ that you build around your
own heart that robs you of the joys of others blessing you. Bitter Root Judgments cause us to "trample
on" even the best intentions of others.

Biblical Example: I Samuel 18 — King Saul with David

What wall of bitterness is your heart hiding
behind?

Healing begins with accepting responsibility for your own
beliefs and judgments and not by blaming others for what
happened/happens.

2. Four common characteristics of bitter root judgments:

a. All things produce after their own kind. We reap what we sow. The seeds we sow multiply. Blessings naturally produce blessings. Curses produce curses. And _____ naturally produce more judgments.

> *"Do not be deceived. God is not mocked, for whatever a man sows, this he will also reap."*
> **Galatians 6:7 (NASV)**

b. The longer a judgment continues in a person's life, the more _____ takes hold. The seeds of judgment may seem tiny when you look back on your childhood experiences, but when you hold on to that judgment into your adulthood it can grow and multiply many times.

> *"Do not judge or you too will be judged. For in the same way you judge others, you will be judged, and with the measure you use, it will be measured to you."*
> **Matthew 7:1-2 (NIV)**

c. Bitter Root Judgments are like strong _____ in your life. Whatever judgments you have, you will be drawn to others who possess the same characteristics as your judgments. In this manner not only will your judgments be fulfilled, but they will also be strengthened.

Examples: All men are jerks, thus men will be jerks around you.

Most troubled marriages are the result of Bitter Root Judgments that have never been dealt with in the life of each partner.

What you believe is most often what you will receive.

   d. Bitter Root Judgments are like

        _____.

3. Forgiveness is always *the* key to
    _____. You need to forgive the
individual involved when the bitter root attached. You
will also need to seek forgiveness for the sin of making
the judgment.

> *"But if you do not forgive men their sins, your
> Father will not forgive your sins."*
>
> **Matthew 6:15**
>
> *"And whenever you stand praying, if you find that
> you carry something in your heart against another
> person, release him and forgive him so that your
> Father in heaven will also release you and forgive
> you of your faults."*
>
> **Mark 11:25**
>
> *"So then, if you are presenting a gift before the
> altar in the temple and suddenly you remember a
> quarrel you have with a fellow believer, leave your
> gift there in front of the altar and go at once to
> apologize with the one who is offended. Then, after
> you have reconciled, come to the altar and present
> your gift."*
>
> **Matthew 5:23-24**

4. One of the blessings that come with breaking inner vows and Bitter Root Judgments is that the cycle is _____. Changes will take place. Sometimes the changes will be subtle, and at other times more dramatic.

   a. As your beliefs are conformed to God's Word by the _____ of your mind, the things that use to bother and irritate you will now _____ of you.

   b. As your beliefs are turned from deception to _____, you are one step closer to being conformed into the image of your Lord Jesus Christ and producing the fruit of the Spirit.

What Bitter Root Judgments are you willing to break in order to renew your mind and grow in the fruit of the Spirit?

Note that Bitter Root Judgments are absolutes. It's either all or nothing. There's very little room for grace, mercy, and forgiveness. Some common Bitter Root Judgments are:

❏ Others are to make me happy.
❏ No one respects me.
❏ If I tell the truth people will be angry with me.
❏ No one trusts me.
❏ No one ever wants to hear what I have to say.
❏ No one really cares…
❏ People in authority will hurt you (or take advantage of you).
❏ All women (or men) are controlling.
❏ God doesn't hear me.
❏ Men (or women) only want one thing.
❏ No one needs me.
❏ If you give someone an inch they'll take a mile.
❏ God doesn't care.
❏ No one likes me (wants to be my friend).
❏ Others see my sin (or shame).
❏ Everyone thinks I'm stupid.
❏ Everyone thinks I'm ugly.
❏ Friends never remain faithful.
❏ Others always end up rejecting me.

- ❏ Others won't allow me in.
- ❏ Everyone looks down on me.
- ❏ Relationships never last.
- ❏ Everyone lies.
- ❏ People (and God) won't forgive me.
- ❏ Everyone else gets the breaks.
- ❏ Others don't see my worth (value).
- ❏ White people can't dance.
- ❏ If I share my heart it will be broken.
- ❏ All Christians are hypocrites.
- ❏ No one sees my loneliness.
- ❏ You're never satisfied.
- ❏ No one will ever love me again.
- ❏ Everyone sees my confusion.

5. How to break Bitter Root Judgments
   a. Identify the event or person in your life that caused you to make the Bitter Root Judgment. Go back to the first time you recall thinking/making your judgment.
   b. Go through the healing process of the event/events that brought you to make the judgment by recalling and then releasing your pain to Jesus.
   c. Choose to forgive the person/people involved.
   d. Ask God to forgive you for passing the judgments.
   e. Sever the judgment with the Sword of the Spirit.
   f. Confess the Bitter Root Judgment and break its hold in the name of Jesus Christ.
   g. Choose to believe the Truth that God gave you in exchange.
   h. Pronounce a blessing on the offender. Romans 12:14 says to "Bless those who persecute you; bless and do not curse."

Bitter Root Judgment I want to deal with:

_____

_____

_____

_____

_____

Before we do the healing prayer, I want you to say: *Holy Spirit, please show me the pain that this Bitter Root Judgment has cost me in my life.*

_____

_____

_____

_____

Holy Spirit, show me if I am suffering from any physical disease due to my bitter root judgments?

_____

_____

_____

Sample Healing Prayer

In the name of Jesus Christ I confess I have carried the Bitter Root Judgment of _____(judgment)_____. I release my pain of _____(specify the pain)_____ and give it to you, Jesus. Jesus, what will you give me in exchange for that pain?

_____

_____

_____

Thank you Jesus, I receive that. I forgive _____(name)_____ for the way they treated me. In Jesus Christ's name, I command complete healing and restoration of _____(disease)_____ caused by my bitter root judgment. By Your stripes I am healed. Thank you Jesus. Please Jesus forgive me for my judgment. I break the power of the Bitter Root Judgment of _____(judgment)_____ in my life. In the name of Jesus Christ, I sever the judgment with the Sword of the Spirit. I turn my back on this judgment. I renounce any demonization that exists as a result of my judgment. Jesus, what is the Truth from your word about my Bitter Root Judgement?_____(the Truth)_____ I choose now to believe_____(the Truth)_____ . I ask a blessing on _____(name)_____ who hurt and offended me.

Breakthrough Declarations

1. I sow good seeds and attract positive people to my life (Galatians 6:7).

2. I am not easily offended (Matthew 7:1-2; Hebrews 2:15).

3. I forgive others quickly and what used to bother me rolls off easily (Mark 11:25).

4. I believe the best of others (Philippians 2:3; 4:8).

5. I will bless others and not curse them (Romans 12:14).

Personal Application

Check any of the Bitter Root Judgments that apply to you (on page 72). Pray for the Holy Spirit to identify any other Bitter Root Judgments in your life (that may not be on the list). Pray through the steps of breaking each of those judgments.

You may want to make a list of your judgments as well as the Truth as a reminder to you:

My Bitter Root Judgments: The Truth:

_____   _____

_____   _____

_____   _____

_____   _____

_____   _____

_____   _____

_____   _____

Use additional pages if you need more room.

Fill-in-the-Blank Answer Guide

1. others   me
   a. stronghold
   b. bitterness
2. a. judgments
   b. bitterness
   c. magnets
   d. lassos
3. healing
4. broken
   a. renewing   roll off
   b. Truth

Personal Notes

_____

_____

_____

_____

_____

_____

_____

_____

_____

_____

_____

_____

_____

_____

_____

_____

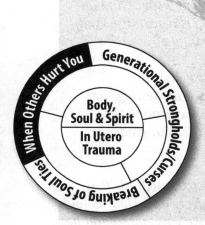

Body,
Soul & Spirit

In Utero
Trauma

Generational Strongholds/Curses

When Others Hurt You

Breaking of Soul Ties

6

When Others Hurt You Intentionally or Unintentionally

When our oldest son Bryan was in the 3rd grade, the teacher came to us at the fall Parent-Teacher Conference and suggested that we have Bryan tested by the school psychologist for a possible reading disability. While Bryan read at grade level, he did poorly on the reading comprehension tests

We agreed and three months later we met with school psychologist, teacher, principal, Jim and I. He told us he had good news and bad news. The good news was that Bryan tested average in everything. The potential bad news was that Bryan was off-task a lot. He stood when his classmates were sitting. I just chalked it up to him being an active boy.

The doctor said he didn't know for sure but he thinks Bryan may have Attention Deficit Disorder. Prior to that declaration, Jim and I had always jokingly said that ADD is really Discipline Deficit Disorder...until it was our son. I went into my control mode and took out books from the library, read everything I could find on the Internet and quickly surmised that ADD is hereditary. Well, we certainly knew Bryan didn't get ADD from me!

In 5th grade, we had Bryan tested by a top Pediatric Neuropsychologist and he confirmed through his testing that Bryan was indeed ADD. He recommended medication. We resisted and tried everything else. Finally after 7th grade we medicated him.

But, beginning in 4th grade and all the way through his first year of college, Bryan was bullied almost every day. He was told he was stupid and annoying... every day. He was cursed and he became what they said he was. That was years before I learned about curses. Now I know that when we jokingly said starting when he was about five years old that "well, Bryan has to learn all his lessons the hard way" we were actually cursing him unintentionally. When I learned this lesson about curses and blessings, I apologized to Bryan and had him break that curse over his life.

Nationwide research indicates that about 20% of students ages 12-18 experienced bullying. Bullying affects all youth, including those who are bullied, those who bully others, and those who witness bullying. The effects of bullying may continue into adulthood.

Bullying is a form of cursing others and it results in hurts that live on into adulthood. It changes one's belief system. If you receive what others say about you as a child in to your soul (your mind, will, emotions), you'll walk it out in your life unless you learn how to break those curses (which hurt you). That is what we talk about in this lesson.

> *"May those who bless you be blessed and those who curse you be cursed!"*
>
> **Numbers 24:9b**

> *"but the tongue is not able to be tamed. It's a fickle, unrestrained evil that spews out words full of toxic poison! We use our tongue to praise God our Father and then turn around and curse a person who was made in his very image! Out of the same mouth we pour out words of praise one minute and curses the next. My brothers and sister, this should never be!*
>
> **James 3:8-10**

Y̶ou know from the Bible that there is power in the tongue—life and death are in your words. This lesson is written to help you break the curses that have been spoken over you (intentionally or unintentionally) or that you have spoken over others.

1. To curse is primarily an Old Testament concept. It is a
   _____ _____ meant to release negative spiritual
   power against the object, person, or place being cursed.
   a. Three times God declares He will curse the one who
      curses His people. Read Numbers 24:9 (above).
   b. Noah pronounced a curse on Canaan and a blessing
      on Shem and Japheth (Genesis 9:25-27)
   c. Isaac blesses his twin sons and pronounces a curse
      upon anyone who would want to curse Jacob.
      (Genesis 27)

The power released in either blessing or cursing was considered _____. The curse was to be feared and the blessing to coveted.

---

2. Current day curses may be pronounced by:
   a. Someone who continues to speak _____ words over you or about you. For instance, "You are stupid". The more it is said, it takes on a stronghold over your soul.

   b. Intercessors may _____ pray and actually speak a curse over someone. For example, praying that God would burn down the porno store instead of praying for redemption.

   c. A person claiming someone as his or her spouse when there is no mutual interest is pronouncing a curse of _____ on that person.

   d. Can Christians curse other Christians? _____.

To curse a man is to curse God (see James 3:9 as man is made in God's image)

"With the tongue we praise our Lord and Father, and with it we curse men, who have been made in God's likeness."

James 3:9 (NIV)

ROOTS		FRUIT
	determine	*influences*
Your Thoughts ⟶	**How You Feel** ⟶	**What You Do**
(Mind)	(Emotions)	(Will/Choices)

satan lies to you   *impacts your*

⟹ **SEED**
(Trauma/Wounds/Curses)   Circumstances

The 1828 Webster's Dictionary defines curse as "To utter a wish of evil against another. To inflict or torment or bring condemnation."

T Lewis and R.K. Harrison (in *The Handbook for Spiritual Warfare* by Dr. Ed Murphy) inform us: *"When a curse is pronounced against any person we are not to understand this as a mere wish, however violent, that disaster should overtake the person in question any more than we are to understand that a corresponding "blessing" conveys a simply a wish that prosperity should be the lot of the person on whom the blessing is involved. A curse was considered to posses an inherent power for carrying itself into effect ... Such curses (and Blessings) possess power."*

3. God has called us to be a people of _____. Wisdom tells us to pay attention to curses sent or spoken over us. They can take on a demonic power that will hinder one from moving in _____.

4. Holiness is a key to our protection. In Numbers 23, Balak used divination to send curses to Israel. But, Balak did not understand that the _____ of a person is a means of protection against evil. What Balam told Balak there is no gate or opportunity for the curses he sent to take root.

> *"He has not observed iniquity in Jacob, nor has He seen wickedness in Israel. The LORD his God is with him, and the shout of a King is among them. God brings them out of Egypt; He has strength like a wild ox. For there is no sorcery against Jacob, nor any divination against Israel. It now must be said of Jacob and of Israel, 'Oh, what God has done!'"*
> **Numbers 23:21-23** (NKJV)

5. Who might possibly curse or intentionally hurt you?

   a. Curses from religious cult groups: Some religious cult groups pray multiple times each day. Those prayers stir the heavens of oppression—words have power that can release the forces of _____.

   We are in a spiritual _____ so be prepared to pray daily against those prayers of false religions who declare that we are their enemies. You may want to pray "In the name and blood of Jesus Christ, I cancel every curse sent over me by ungodly prayers."

   b. Curses from the occult

   "Then Pharaoh also called the wise men and sorcerers: now the magicians of Egypt, the also did in like manner with their enchantments."
   Exodus 7:11

   • These "wise men" are people whose practical advice is based upon _____ revelation (see Jeremiah 50:35; Ezekiel 27:9, Obadiah 8).
   These "wise men" practiced magic and divination. Their revelation was from other gods instead of the true God of Israel.
   • The word "sorcerer" comes from the Hebrew word *kashaph* which means "to whisper a _____ _____; to use songs of magic; to mutter magical words of incantations; to enchant; to practice magic; to be a sorcerer; to use witchcraft. They were known to have power from evil spirits.
   • "Magician" is from the Hebrew word *chartom*. Here it means Egyptian or Babylonian sages and magicians who practiced the _____, sorcery, and incantations.

- The Hebrew word for "enchantment" is *lahat*. It means something covered up by the use of secret arts and _____.

As we understand the meaning of the above words, it will help us understand the significance of the occult practices today. There is nothing new under the sun.

    c. Unintentional "friendly-fire" curses include:
- Personal curses of oppression—curses sent over our:
  Body/Health—spoken by health care professionals
  Finances
  Marriage
- Curses from _____ figures including parents, teachers, pastors, etc.
- Curses in the _____ – gossip, prayer

These words have a _____ _____ on the soul and can become strongholds that prevent a person from believing in him/herself.

6. When Moses went to Pharaoh to see the release of the Israelites, he went under the _____ of God. There were several curses that the magicians could perform, but they finally gave up and said Moses must be sent from God.

The great news for all believers is that the curses against them could not bring _____ to God's people.

> *"For our struggle is not against flesh and blood, but against the rulers, against the authorities, against the powers of this dark world and against the spiritual forces of evil in the heavenly realms."*
> **Ephesians 6:12**

7. What are the symptoms of being cursed?

    a. Oppression is the main one. It is a _____ that seems to be surrounding you.

    b. _____ can be caused by curses in particular areas such as heart attacks, back pain, headaches, etc.

    c. Curses may be sent over your _____ . What better way to limit the influence of the church than to limit the money coming into the church through tithes and offerings.

    d. Curses may be sent to Christian families to destroy the _____ of the leaders.

    e. Curses are sent upon the _____ and areas specifically where there are churches working toward reconciliation between races. Satan wants division not unity. Example: Tecumseh and Chillicothe

8. How to Break Curses Sent by Others:

First, You need to understand the Power of the Cross. Only when you understand the cross do you understand the power of the Blood. Placing the cross in prayer between you and an area of sin is a type of symbolic or visual prayer. If the cross is between you and the sin, then you have to go back through the cross to pick the sin up again.

> *"Christ redeemed us from that self-defeating, cursed life by absorbing it completely into himself. Do you remember the Scripture that says, "Cursed is everyone who hangs on a tree"? That is what happened when Jesus was nailed to the cross: He became a curse, and at the same time dissolved the curse."*
>
> **Galatians 3:13 The Message**

Second, pronounce in the Name of Jesus Christ that the curse be broken. Be sure to speak the curse by name.

Third, command all that had been taken by the enemy to be restored, plus sevenfold more.

> *"Yet if he (the thief) is caught, he must pay sevenfold though it costs him all the wealth of his house."*
>
> **Proverbs 6:31**

Fourth, forgive the person who sent the curse. You do not need to know who sent the curse, just pronounce forgiveness. If the curse has taken a strong root in you, then you need to spend time with the Lord to find out what sin in your life has allowed the curse to become a stronghold. Seek forgiveness and choose not to walk in whatever area of sin God may reveal.

Fifth, seal the healing with the Blood of Jesus Christ.

 Is there any problem areas that you are dealing with that could be the result of a curse? Then pray about that area and ask the Holy Spirit to reveal if this is actually a curse.

Ask God to reveal to you any curse that has been placed on the land where you live. If there is a curse, break it and ask God to bring forth His blessings upon the land.

Sample Healing Prayer to Break a Curse Over You

Ask Jesus: What pain has this caused me in my life?

_____

_____

_____

Show me if I am suffering from any physical or emotional disease due to curses spoken over me?

_____

_____

_____

In Jesus Christ's name, I break the power of any curse of _____ (curse)_____ that has been spoken against me. I cancel the assignment of the words/prayers. I release the pain to you Jesus that this curse has caused me_____(pain)_____. In Jesus Christ's name, I command complete healing and restoration of _____(disease)_____ caused by this curse. By Your stripes I am healed. Thank you Jesus.

> **¹⁰Now my beloved ones, I have saved these most important truths for last: Be supernaturally infused with strength through your life-union with the Lord Jesus. Stand victorious with the force[a] of his explosive power flowing in and through you. ¹¹ Put on God's complete set of armor provided for us, so that you will be protected as you fight against the evil strategies of the accuser! ¹²Your hand-to-hand combat is not with human beings, but with the highest principalities and authorities**

operating in rebellion under the heavenly realms. For they are a powerful class of demon gods and evil spirits that hold this dark world in bondage. ¹³Because of this, you must wear all the armor that God provides so you're protected as you confront the slanderer, for you are destined for all things and will rise victorious.

¹⁴Put on truth as a belt to strengthen you to stand in triumph. Put on holiness as the protective armor that covers your heart. ¹⁵Stand on your feet alert, then you'll always be ready to share the blessings of peace.

¹⁶In every battle, take faith as your wrap around shield, for it is able to extinguish the blazing arrows coming at you from the Evil One. ¹⁷⁻¹⁸Embrace the power of salvation's full deliverance, like a helmet to protect your thoughts from lies. And take the mighty razor-sharp Spirit sword of the spoken Word of God.

Pray passionately in the Spirit, as you constantly intercede with every form of prayer at all times. Pray the blessings of God upon all his believers.

Ephesians 6:10-18

9. Exposing the _____ of the devil weakens him while at the same time empowering the believer for _____ . We can do nothing with our heads buried in the sand of apathy. Or, we can take our positions in God's army ready to move into battle.

We can hold back the darkness by walking more boldly in the light on a daily basis. Commit to becoming an active warrior in battling the forces of darkness against your family, your community, this nation, and the world.

> *"And the Lord shall make you the head, and not the tail; and you shall be above only, and you shall not be beneath, if you heed the commandments of the Lord your God which I command you this day and are watchful to do them."*
> **Deuteronomy 28:13 The Message**

 Now for the rest of the story from Bryan on his College Admissions Essay (written his junior year of high school):

Some people find out who they truly are at a young age. Others find out who they are when they are in high school. And some find out who they are in college. Some never find out who they truly are. I found who I truly am after an ongoing experience in elementary, middle school and early high school.

Throughout my school career, I was not very good with social skills. I was what kids call "different" Usually when watching a movie, viewers can always pick out the kid who is different. The different kid was the one who always gets bullied and pushed around. Unfortunately, I was that "different kid", I didn't' fit in with many of the kids at school. At school, I would space off and blurt out random and often irrelevant ideas and thoughts. I was bullied and made fun of in some of the worst ways. Some days it got so bad that I would come home from school crying. On top of being bullied, my grades started to slip, and my parents started to worry about me. I went to a neuropsychologist and was diagnosed with Attention Deficit Disorder in fifth grade. My parents started me on medicine after seventh grade and my family thought that everything would be fine. I thought I could finally fit in with other kids. I didn't want another year to be yet another terrible year of trying to fit in. This wish, this hope of trying to fit in, continued to be my dream through most of middle school. I focused on getting out of middle school so I could have a fresh start in high school.

I soon realized in ninth grade that I was terribly wrong. What happened to me in fifth grade happened to me in a more seriously traumatizing way. I started high school at an all boys preparatory school, so I would be able to get into a good college. The guys there saw me as a target, and soon I was at one of the lowest points in my life. It was cruel and unusual punishment. One of the guys there would make fun of me and then spit in his hand and throw it at me. I felt as though I was less than human. At this point of my life, I felt like I was being bullied to no return. The bullying and hate left a lasting impression on me that would change my life, as I know it now.

Because of all the tough times I have endured, I have gained a lot of empathy for people with problems. Although I have been through a lot and hate the fact I had to go through it, I have learned I could help people for good with my empathy. Today, friends come to me with their problems. I have discovered some friends have been through relationship problems and bullying themselves. They call me and or I have met up with them in the late hours of the evening to talk and comfort them. They know I have been through so much and that I can relate and help them through everything that is happening to them. In a way, I am in great debt to all the people who have hurt me and subsequently have given me the strength of empathy. I have learned at a young age that even though bad things happen, one can overcome them and become a better person. That's why I feel the need to become a teacher and role model.

Indeed, Bryan graduated cum laude and earned his Early Childhood teaching degree from Ashland University. He has an amazing gift with young children and uses that empathy to work with underprivileged students.

Breakthrough Declarations

1. When I'm upset or hurt, I do not react with anger (Matthew 5:21-22).

2. As I speak God's promises, they come to pass. They stop all attacks, assaults, oppression, and fear from my life (2 Peter 1:2-4; Mark 11:23-24).

3. Any adversity, attack, accidents and tragedies that were headed my way are diverted right now in Jesus' name (Psalm 91).

4. Now I speak to every mountain of fear, every mountain of discouragement, every mountain of stress, every mountain of depression, every mountain of lack and insufficiency; and I say, "Be removed & cast into the sea in Jesus name!" (Mark 11:22-24).

5. I live under a supernatural protection (Psalm 91).

* Some declarations used with permission of Steve and Wendy Backlund with IgnitingHope.com

Additional Reading

The Handbook for Spiritual Warfare, Dr. Ed Murphy, Thomas Nelson Publishers, 1992.

You may want to make a list of the curses you have broken over yourself as well as the curses you have broken that you have spoken over others. This will serve as a reminder to your inner healing progress:

Others' Curses Over Me
I Have Broken:

Curses I Have Broken
Over Others:

_____   _____

_____   _____

_____   _____

_____   _____

_____   _____

_____   _____

_____   _____

_____   _____

_____   _____

_____   _____

_____   _____

_____   _____

_____   _____

_____   _____

_____   _____

_____   _____

_____   _____

_____   _____

_____   _____

_____   _____

Use additional pages if you need more room.

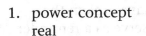

1. power concept
    real
2. a. negative
    b. incorrectly
    c. bondage
    d. yes
3. prayer
    destiny
4. righteousness
5   a. evil   battle
    b. divine
        magic spell
        occult
        tricks
    c. authority
        church
    demonic power
6. anointing
    defeat
7. a. heaviness
    b. sickness
    c. finances
    d. children
    e. land
9. schemes
    battle

Resource: Bullying Research from: https://www.stopbullying.gov/resources/facts

Freedom Beyond Generational Limits/ Curses

I went through a deep inner healing and deliverance session where I learned that I had some very deeply rooted demonic holds in my life that I had no control over. I didn't do anything to invite them in but they had been there from the time I was conceived. It explained why I continued to have a wall around my heart that prevented me from fully loving others and from them loving me.

The same was true of my parent from whom I inherited these generational strongholds. Sometimes, the church or leaders can place undue pressure or guilt on us when we struggle in an area no matter how hard we attempt to deal with it. In my case, my generational curse was a critical nature and being judgmental towards others as well as an intense need to be in control. But God…can break off any generational curse so that we can walk in true freedom. That is my invitation to you in this lesson.

So far in this Bible Study you have learned primarily about strongholds/curses/hurts that you have direct control over. In this lesson, you will learn about curses that existed before you were born. You may have been drawn to certain sins and never understood why. In this lesson you will learn how to have victory over generational sins.

1. What are strongholds? Anything that prevents you from:
    a. truly _____ the Lord
    b. walking in the _____ and _____ that God desires for you.

> **"The weapons of warfare are not carnal, but mighty through God to the pulling down of strongholds: Casting down imaginations and every high thing that exalts itself against the knowledge of God and bringing into captivity every thought to the obedience of Christ."**
>
> **2 Corinthians 10: 4-5**

2. What is the Biblical basis for generational curses?

> **"For I, the Lord your God, am a jealous God, visiting the iniquity of the fathers upon the children to the third and fourth generation of those who hate me, but showing love to a thousand generations of those who love me and keep my commandments."**
>
> **Deuteronomy 5: 9b-10**

> *"Behold I was brought forth in iniquity, and in sin did my mother conceive me."*
>
> **Psalms 51: 5**

3. Three ways generational curses/strongholds may enter your life:
   a. At the time of _____ (original sin).
   b. Through your _____ .
   c. By _____ the sin patterns of your parents.

Examples: Genesis 12: 10-20 Abram and Sarai
             Genesis 26: 7 Isaac and Rebekah
             Genesis 27 Jacob and Esau

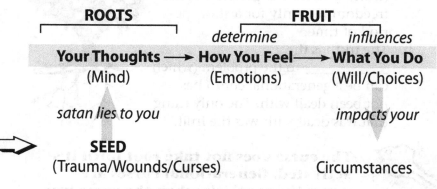

ROOTS   **FRUIT**

determine   *influences*

Your Thoughts ⟶ **How You Feel** ⟶ **What You Do**
(Mind)   (Emotions)   (Will/Choices)

satan lies to you   *impacts your*

SEED
(Trauma/Wounds/Curses)   Circumstances

4. Generational Sin Patterns can be thought of like a _____ _____ in your life.
   a. The generational curse is like the bulb.
   b. The sin pattern is like the stem.

The sin pattern actually produces the right conditions for the fruit to be produced. The fruit is the part of the problem that is produced by sin and can often be seen above the surface or in your actions/behavior.

"By their fruit you will recognize them. Do people pick grapes from thornbushes, or figs from thistles? Likewise every good tree bears good fruit, but a bad tree bears bad fruit. A good tree cannot bear bad fruit, and a bad tree cannot bear good fruit. Every tree that does not bear good fruit is cut down and thrown into the fire. Thus, by their fruit you will recognize them."

Matthew 7:16-20

5. Why only "picking the fruit" doesn't work . . .

a. If you only change your behavior (fruit), you may experience some freedom but only for a short period of time.

b. The truth is the _____ _____ to the problem (which can be a generational curse) has not been dealt with. The only thing that was dealt with was the fruit.

The curse does not take root until it's activated. Generational curses are never the root. It's when the curse was activated that it became rooted in you. In order for complete inner healing to take place, you must first deal with the root issue, then deal with the sin pattern. What was your memory that first activated the curse?

_____

_____

_____

_____

_____

_____

Remember, the curse itself is what creates certain tendencies and desires. Your own choice to sin is then what actives the curse. It's always your own choice to choose obedience or to sin.

More Biblical Examples of Blessings and Curses

The 27th and the 28th chapters of the book of Deuteronomy are chapters about blessings and curses. Listed below you will find some of the *basic areas* which cause curses, along with some of the *basic effects* of curses:

Basic Areas of Curses:

Deuteronomy 27:16-17	Finances
27:16	Rebellion
27:17	Dishonesty
27:18	Cruelty
27:19	Taking unfair advantage
27:20-23	Sexual
27:24-25	Violence
Malachi 3:8-9	Robbing God

Basic Effects of Curses:

Deuteronomy 28:16-17	Finances
28:18	Fruit of the womb
28:19	Home
28:20	Confusion (mental illness)
28:21-22	Sickness and disease
28:23	Unanswered prayer
28:24	Land/drought
28:25, 30-34	Defeat
28:35	Disease
28:36-37	Enslaved to evil
28:38-40	Labor of hands not prosper
28:41	Broken Relationships
28:43-44	Poverty

6. Understanding generational curses and sin

    a. God's laws (His directions and instructions) are to
       _____ us and _____ us from being
       harmed by the effects of sin.

    b. A generational curse is caused by the effects of sin
       and is a consequence of _____.

    c. Jesus stopped the _____ of your sin by
       becoming a curse for you and dying on the cross to
       redeem you.

When Jesus Christ died on the cross he stopped the judgment of sin in our lives. Jesus redeemed us through the shedding of His blood so that the blessings of Abraham might come to the Gentiles through Him.

> *"Christ redeemed us from the curse of the law by becoming a curse for us, for it is written: 'cursed is everyone who is hung on a tree.' "*
> **Galatians 3:13** (NIV)

We no longer need to reap the judgments of generational curses because Christ has shed His blood for us. Through the death and resurrection of Jesus Christ, the judgment of sin has already been paid for. That is, if you have accepted Jesus Christ into your heart as your Lord and your Savior.

> *"In fact the law requires that nearly everything be cleansed with blood and without the shedding of blood there is no forgiveness."*
> **Hebrews 9:22** (NIV)

d. Jesus did not stop the _____ of sin.

Sometimes sin breaks things when it's not even intentional. But sin can always be forgiven. It will not change God's love for you. The consequences of sin still have to be dealt with so the effects of sin aren't passed down for generations becoming a sin pattern.

Discussion Question: Can you think of any generational sin patterns that easily come to mind from your extended family? Perhaps there is divorce, early death, substance abuse, children conceived before marriage, lying or deception, gambling, obesity, sexual sins, cult or occult sins, etc. *Please don't share any names*. What generational sin patterns can you identify in your own family?

_____

_____

_____

_____

_____

_____

_____

_____

_____

_____

_____

_____

_____

_____

7. Your personal responsibility – it's all about choice!

   a. When you break a generational curse, it is still your responsibility to walk away from any _____ _____ in your life.

   b. You must choose to walk in Truth and to realign your beliefs, values, desires, and actions to the Truth of God's Word.

   c. You always have a _____. If you chose to walk in obedience, then your choice will cause blessings to be passed down a thousand generations.

> *"See, I set before you today life and prosperity, death and destruction. For I command you today to love the LORD your God, to walk in his ways, and to keep his commands, decrees and laws; then you will live and increase, and the LORD your God will bless you in the land you are entering to possess. But if your heart turns away and you are not obedient, and if you are drawn away to bow down to other gods and worship them, I declare to you this day that you will certainly be destroyed. You will not live long in the land you are crossing the Jordan to enter and possess. This day I call heaven and earth as witnesses against you that I have set before you life and death, blessings and curses. Now choose life, so that you and your children may live."*
>
> **Deuteronomy 30: 15-19**

Sample Healing Prayer to Break Generational Curses

*In the Name of Jesus Christ, I identify the sin pattern of*_____(name one at a time)_____*. I forgive the past generations for walking in this particular sin and for bringing judgment/pain on me (and my family). I seek forgiveness for all the way(s) I have walked in the sin pattern. I break the power of the generational curse of*_____(name curse)_____*in the Name and by the Blood of Jesus Christ and I place the cross of Jesus Christ between the curse and myself*. I renounce any level of demonization that exists as a result of this generational curse. I make the choice to walk away from that sin and walk in obedience†. Amen*

*Add if applies: I also forgive*_____(name)_____*who abused me in this area.*

* Placing the cross in prayer between you and an area of sin is a type of symbolic or visual prayer. If the cross is between you and the sin, then you have to go back through the cross to pick the sin up again.

† This may mean not to drink alcohol, buy pornographic materials, or whatever else the sin may be.

DON'T KEEP THE SECRET!

8. Generational blessings – example Ruth the Moabite

> *"...but showing love to a thousand generations of those who love me and keep my commandments."*
> **Deuteronomy 5: 10** (NIV)

A generational blessing is so much _____ than a generational curse. Reverse the curses in your own life. Ruth chose to do this in her life, and you can see the results.

God desires that you walk in the fullness of His blessings, and that you reverse every generational curse in your life. Your heavenly Father's heart toward you is that you begin to walk in the generational blessings He so much desires for you and your descendants to walk in.

Discussion Questions:

1. Turn to the book of Ruth and identify some of her choices that ultimately blessed her and her family. What lessons can we learn from Ruth?

_____

_____

_____

_____

_____

_____

2. What family blessings have you seen passed down through your family's generations? How have those impacted you? How have you sought to pass those down to your children?

_____

_____

_____

_____

_____

_____

Remember, it is your choice to choose life!

Breakthrough Declarations

1. God redeemed me from all generational curses (Galatians 3:13). I walk in faith and bear good fruit (Matthew 7:16-20).

2. I walk in godly patterns in my life choosing life and blessings (Deuteronomy 30:19).

3. I have a covenant with God, and by the blood of Jesus I release my divine protection and divine provision (Hebrews 8:6).

4. And I speak to this day and I call you blessed. And I declare that I serve a mighty God who today will do exceedingly and abundantly beyond all that I can ask or think (Ephesians 3:20). I say you are a good God and I eagerly anticipate your goodness today.

5. Each of my family members is wonderfully blessed and radically loves Jesus (Acts 16:30-31).

* Some declarations used with permission of Steve and Wendy Backlund with IgnitingHope.com

Personal Application:

Look at your family lineage. On your father's side of the family what sin patterns do you see which may have been passed down from generation to generation?

My own sibling(s) weaknesses/failures

_____

_____

_____

Father

_____

_____

_____

Grandpa and Grandma

_____

_____

_____

Great Grandpas and Grandmas

_____

_____

Great Great Grandpas and Grandmas

_____

_____

Action Steps

1. Forgive each person for walking in any area of sin that God revealed to you and for passing down a generational curse. Do not make your prayers general. Be as specific as you can.
2. Ask for forgiveness if you have also walked in this same area of sin.
3. Use the Prayer on page 101 to break these curses in your life.

Look at your family lineage. On your mother's side of the family what sin patterns do you see which may have been passed down from generation to generation?

Mother

_____

_____

_____

Grandpa and Grandma

_____

_____

Great Grandpas and Grandmas

_____

_____

Great Great Grandpas and Grandmas

_____

_____

Action Steps
1. Forgive each person for walking in any area of sin that God revealed to you and for passing down a generational curse. Do not make your prayers general. Be as specific as you can.
2. Ask for forgiveness if you have also walked in this same area of sin.
3. Use the Prayer on page 69 to break these curses in your life.

My Personal Tree Application Page

For those who prefer a visual representation of your own tree and its potential impact on your children, this is an excellent tool for you. It may also help you to explain generational curses to your children with this page. Please follow these steps:

1. Write in your own fruit – both good (kind, generous, hardworker, etc.) and bad (procrastinator, sexual immorality, workaholic, etc.) on the tree.
2. Write down the fruit or weaknesses and/or failures that you see in your siblings.
3. After completing the exercises on pages 104-105, write in the generational curses in your family. Add as many lines as are necessary.
4. Pray through the healing prayer on page 101. Help your children complete this assignment and walk them through the healing prayer as well (they must break their own generational curses, you cannot do it for them unless they are babies).

_____'s Tree

My Fruit (Good and Bad):

My Siblings' Weaknesses/ Failures/Strengths:

Generational Curses/Sins/Habits/Blessings:

Personal Victory Journal of Your Healing Progress

 You may want to make a list of the Generational Curses you have broken as a reminder to your inner healing progress:

Generational Curses I Have Broken:

_____   _____
_____   _____
_____   _____
_____   _____
_____   _____
_____   _____
_____   _____
_____   _____
_____   _____
_____   _____

Use additional pages if you need more room.

Generational Blessings I Am Thankful For:

_____   _____
_____   _____
_____   _____
_____   _____
_____   _____
_____   _____
_____   _____
_____   _____
_____   _____

Use additional pages if you need more room.

1. loving, victory, blessings
3. a. conception
   b. genes
   c. walking in
4. tulip bulb
5. root issue
6. a. protect, prevent
   b. disobedience
   c. judgment
   d. pattern
7. a. sin patterns
   c. choice
8. stronger

Breaking Unhealthy Soul Ties

Like many couples prior to marriage, Jim and I petted heavily but never had intercourse. I felt guilty about that and the switch from no, no, no to YES now that we were married was extremely challenging for me. That was unexpected but no one really talked to me about sex so I didn't know what to expect or how to respond. Sex was a taboo subject in our home growing up and most certainly in our church.

Jim thought it would be helpful for us to watch soft porn together. I didn't know he even looked at porn at the time nor did I know anything about it. He was exposed to Playboy magazine as a boy scout. I thought it couldn't hurt, but little did I know that I was tying my soul and sexual satisfaction to pornography and not my husband. More guilt ensued. Reading romance novels as a teenager and into adulthood also planted the seed of lust in my life.

After a couple of years, I went through a pornography recovery program that stopped me from looking at porn but I still used those past images to come to an orgasm. Then a friend shared at our Bible Study group how she got get rid of bad memories (including trauma). This was absolutely a turning point after years of struggling with porn images. I will share the Scripture and activation later in this lesson.

> **"One final word, friends. We ask you—urge is more like it—that you keep on doing what we told you to do to please God, not in a dogged religious plod, but in a living, spirited dance. You know the guidelines we laid out for you from the Master Jesus. God wants you to live a pure life.**
> **Keep yourselves from sexual promiscuity. Learn to appreciate and give dignity to your body, not abusing it, as is so common among those who know nothing of God.**
> **Don't run roughshod over the concerns of your brothers and sisters. Their concerns are God's concerns, and he will take care of them. We've warned you about this before. God hasn't invited us into a disorderly, unkempt life but into something holy and beautiful—as beautiful on the inside as the outside.**
>
> **I Thessalonians 4:3-7 (The Message)**

S oul ties are emotional bonds that form an attachment. They may be godly or ungodly, pure or demonic. Most people use the term soul tie to refer to connections linking people. Soul ties are not necessarily sexual or romantic. We can form an ungodly attachment with any person, place, or thing. Individuals can be overly attached to pets, possessions, or anything else imaginable:

> *"...You are a slave to whatever controls you"*
>
> **2 Peter 2:19 NLT**

> *They traded the truth about God for a lie. So they worshiped and served the things God created instead of the Creator himself, who is worthy of eternal praise!*
>
> **Romans 1:25 NLT**

God doesn't want our soul in bondage to soul ties that turn our heart away from Him. God desires to restore our soul that we might be able to seek Him with our whole (entire) spirit, soul, and body.... We cannot be obedient to God's command to serve Him with all of our soul if we lack possession of a complete, whole soul! We will begin this lesson with sexual soul ties.

> *"Now may the God of peace Himself sanctify you completely; and may your whole spirit, soul, and body be preserved blameless at the coming of our Lord Jesus Christ"*
>
> **(1 Thessalonians 5:23).**

1. God created us from the very beginning as _____ and _____. He intricately designed us as different genders in order to bring about the beauty of _____ through the blessing of sexual intercourse in marriage.

---

2. We cannot become loving human beings by simply being conceived and born. A person must be nurtured into the ability to truly _____ another person.

   a. The father's role is to _____ that life.

   b. The mother's role is to _____ that life.

   c. Some people who are involved in sex outside of marriage hate or strongly _____ their parents. They use sex as a subconscious way to throw away their parents' rights to rejoice in the child's glory. Women sometimes look to sexual relationships as a means of approval, which they lack from their father.

3. All sexual activity that is not within God's definition _____ the blessings that God intended for man and woman.

   a. Sexual sins come from the _____ of my will and it affects how my spirit relates to God, others, and myself.

   b. Webster's Dictionary defines sex as: anything connected with sexual _____ or arousal or reproduction. By definition, French kissing is sex, foreplay is sex, oral sex is sex, masturbation is sex, etc.

"People conceived and brought into life by God don't make a practice of sin. How could they? God's seed is deep within them, making them who they are. It's not in the nature of the God-begotten to practice and parade sin. Here's how you tell the difference between God's children and the Devil's children: The one who won't practice righteous ways isn't from God, nor is the one who won't love brother or sister. A simple test."

I John 3:9 (The Message)

"There's more to sex than mere skin on skin. Sex is as much spiritual mystery as physical fact. As written in Scripture, "The two become one." Since we want to become spiritually one with the Master, we must not pursue the kind of sex that avoids commitment and intimacy, leaving us more lonely than ever—the kind of sex that can never "become one." There is a sense in which sexual sins are different from all others. In sexual sin we violate the sacredness of our own bodies, these bodies that were made for God-given and God-modeled love, for "becoming one" with another. Or didn't you realize that your body is a sacred place, the place of the Holy Spirit? Don't you see that you can't live however you please, squandering what God paid such a high price for? The physical part of you is not some piece of property belonging to the spiritual part of you. God owns the whole works. So let people see God in and through your body."

I Corinthians 6: 16-20 (The Message)

4. Often people who have committed fornication or adultery will tell you that they fell in love and then out of love. Fornication is sexual intimacy _____ marriage. Adultery _____ the covenant of marriage. Adultery is breaking the 7th commandment.

The reality is that they fell into hate not love.

Fornication and adultery includes manipulating one another for self-pleasure. When a person commits sexual sin, they flaunt all that is holy for selfish reasons. Immorality is ugly and destructive.

No person who is truly a lover ever _____ another. In using others, they demolish the glory of God designed for blessings.

"But my people have exchanged their Glory for worthless idols."

Jeremiah 2:11b (NIV)

5. If you have committed sexual sins, it is important to look for the _____ _____ for the choice you made.

6. Besides healing the root, it is also important to break _____ _____ with your sexual partners.

   a. Any sexual act _____ a person's spirit with the spirit of another.

"Do you not know that he who unites himself with a prostitute is one with her in body? For it is said, "The two will become one flesh."

I Corinthians 6:16

In the sexual act, you become knitted together and your spirit remembers the union. These unions can be thought of as large

_____ _____.

The rubber band is what binds you together, even after the sexual act is over. For each sexual partner there is a different rubber band. If you have many sexual partners, you will experience increasing bondage as the rubber bands tying you to your partners become tighter and tighter.

b. The first sexual union is the most important because a _____ covenant is established when the female's hymen is broken (and bleeds). The only way to break that covenant is the blood covenant of Jesus Christ.

c. If you have been _____ , the demon of rape may harass you because it was taken from you. You will need to break the soul ties with your rapist.

7. Adultery not only breaks the marriage covenant, but also brings upon yourself a curse of _____ (read Numbers 5:11-31). If you divorced your spouse because your spouse committed adultery, you need to deal with the spirit of _____ .

If you do not deal with your jealousy you can carry that into your next relationship. This may cause you to find it difficult to trust in your next relationship.

8. Involvement with _____ is found in the Bible – "poreneuf" is translated as the word "adultery" in Mark 10:19a. Pornography is the "carbon monoxide poisoning" of the church because you can't see it yet it destroys people.

> *"You know the commandments: 'Do not murder, do not commit adultery, do not steal, do not give false testimony, do not defraud, honor your father and mother.'"*
>
> **Mark 10:19**

9. When Jesus forgives He also forgets. For I will demonstrate My mercy to them and will forgive their evil deeds, and never remember again their sins (Hebrews 8:12). According to the Bible, we can do what Jesus does (John 14:12) so you can command those painful

memories to leave you and they must. This has been incredibly powerful in my life for removing porn images and other painful memories. It works. Those scenes disappeared and don't replay in my mind even if I try to remember them. What a blessing! Also read Isaiah 65:16-19. Don't let the enemy torment your soul.

Sample prayer

Thank you Jesus for forgiving and forgetting my sins. I command all remembrance of ___(painful situation)___ to be gone from my memory in the name and blood of Jesus Christ. Remove all memories and shame (list other negative emotions) of this situation from the cellular level of my body in Jesus' name. Thank You Jesus for healing my memories and giving me rest in my soul, body, and spirit.

Commanding those images to go from my memory and break-ing my unhealthy soul tie to pornography was the turning point in my relationship with my husband. Here are two more helpful tips: (1) Before Jim and I are intimate, I submit my spirit, soul, and body to Holy Spirit so that I come to our marriage bed with purity and love. (2) I also read out loud the sample prayer I provide at the end of this chapter.

10. Breaking the Power of Soul Ties:

   a. To break the bondage of oneness you must confess your sexual sins. The Bible states to be specific in our prayers. This means you need to confess your sexual partners by name (first name is fine). If you have been involved with pornography you will not need to use a name of the person but still confess your sin.

   b. You need to seek forgiveness for the sexual act that you just confessed.

   c. Forgive the other person involved.

d. Forgive yourself. This means to accept Christ's forgiveness. What Christ accomplished on the cross for your sins is final as well as complete.

e. If there was a blood covenant (your first sexual experience outside of marriage), break the blood covenant made with the power of the blood covenant of Jesus Christ.†† *(see page 118)*

f. Pray to cut any soul ties between yourself and the person that you had sex with.

g. If you have been sexually molested or raped, follow these guidelines to break the power of oneness with the offender.

h. If you are bitter or jealous, you will want to break that curse as well.* *(see page 118)*

These prayers need to be done with each sexual relationship outside the covenant of marriage. This includes any sexual relationship you had with a future spouse. For individuals that you do not remember their name, still repent and cut those ties.

Holy Spirit, show me if I am suffering from any physical disease due to my unhealthy soul ties?

_____

_____

_____

Sample Healing Prayer to Break Unhealthy Sexual Soul Ties

In the name of Jesus Christ, I break the power of all ungodly sprit, soul and bodily ties between_____(name)_____and me. By the power of the cross, I send back to_____(name)_____ all parts of him/her that s/he gave to me that never belonged to me. And I take back from_____(name)_____all parts of me that I gave to him/her that never belonged to them. Please forgive me for my unhealthy soul tie. I accept Your forgiveness of my sin and Your complete restoration. I forgive_____(name)_____ for their involvement. I choose by an act of my will to forgive myself for my part and I break off any shame and pain from my soul connected to this unhealthy soul tie in Jesus name.

In Jesus Christ's name, I command complete healing and restoration of_____(disease)_____caused by my soul tie(s). By Your stripes I am healed. Thank you Jesus.

Father, I ask you to set a guard over my spirit, soul and body to never again connect with_____(name)_____in any ungodly way. I sever the ties from my soul, spirit, and body. I am free and_____(name)_____is set free. I nail to the cross the lie that joining with_____(name)_____in these ungodly ways was necessary, needed, or wanted on my part. I break all agreements I've made with this soul tie known or unknown and I turn away from joining with it.

Father, as you break this soul tie away from me, what is Your Truth about this situation that you want me to know .

_____

_____

_____

i. †† To break a blood covenant, add: *In the name of Jesus Christ and by the power of His blood, I break the blood covenant with* _____ (name) _____. *This covenant no longer has a hold upon me.*

j.* If bitterness or jealousy was involved, add: *In Jesus Christ's name and by the power of His blood, I break the curse of bitterness (or jealousy) that has entered me because of the adulteress relationship with*_____ (name) _____. *This curse no longer has a hold upon me. I am forgiven.*

Sample Healing Prayer for Unhealthy Non-Sexual Soul Ties

Both prayers dapted from: Erin Lamb https://ithoughtiknewwhatlovewas.com

*In Jesus name, I break any connection of mine to*_____ (name) _____ *in the soul/spirit realm that's not of God. I command any parts of their soul attached to mine to be released back to them cleansed in the blood of Jesus and free of any demonic spirits. I command any spirits not of the Holy Spirit that attached to me or came to me through this bond to leave and go to Jesus never to return to me. I choose by an act of my will to forgive* _____ (name) _____ *and me for my part and I break off any shame and pain from my soul connected to this unhealthy soul tie in Jesus name.*

I ask God for a wall of fire around my soul, spirit, and body so nothing from them not of You passes into me. I call back any parts of my soul linked to them, cleansed in the blood of Jesus and free of any demonic spirits. They are free, and I am free in Jesus name.

Sample Prayer to Use Before Intimacy with a Spouse Who Has Not Yet Done Soul Healing (this protects you from receiving anything not of God from him/her)

God, thank you for my union with my spouse. I thank you for them and our intimacy. I want all the good that flows through my spouse to flow into me. I do not want anything that is not of You to have access to me. I bind any spirits that are not of Your spirit from entering me through our soul tie and covenant.

I am not in agreement with any of my spouse's sin. I break agreement with any of my spouse's sin and command any spirits we share in common to go to a dry uninhabited place. I ask God for a wall of fire around my soul, spirit, and body so nothing from them not of You passes into me.

In the name of Jesus, I break any ungodly portions of my soul tie with my spouse and command any spirits from my spouse to go to a dry uninhabited place, never to return. My soul is a no access area to demons. When we are physically or emotionally intimate, I forbid any spirits from entering my body or soul.

I ask for purifying fire on our union. I pray for the soul healing and restoration of my spouse. Lord may my healing be a catalyst for my spouse's freedom. In Jesus' power name, Amen.

Breakthrough Declarations

1. I am sexually pure and honor God with my body (I Corinthians 6:18-20; I Thessalonians 4:3-7; Hebrews 13:4).

2. God's love and peace is in every relationship I have (Colossians 3:14).

3. I exercise self-control and show love to others (1 Corinthians 13:4-5).

4. I prosper in all my relationships (Luke 2:52).

5. I consistently bring God encounters to other people (Mark 16:17,18).

* Some declarations used with permission of Steve and Wendy Backlund with IgnitingHope.com

Personal Application

Make a list of sexual partners (other than spouse) or sex acts that you need to pray through. Ask the Holy Spirit to reveal any other soul ties that you have made. Ask Holy Spirit to show you any root causes that you need to deal with that caused you to make unhealthy soul ties.

_____

_____

_____

_____

_____

_____

_____

_____

_____

1. male
   female
   oneness
2. love
   a. protect
   b. nurture
   c. disrespect
3. distorts
   a. choices
   b. gratification
4. before
   violates
   uses
5. root cause
6. soul ties
   a. unites
      rubber bands
   b. blood
   c. raped
7. bitterness
   jealousy
8. pornography

Bonus Materials

How Can I Be Saved?

> *"And this is the testimony: God has given us eternal life, and this life is in His Son. He who has the Son has life; he who does not have the Son of God does not have life."*
>
> **1 John 5:11-12** (NIV)

This passage tells us that God has given us eternal life and this life is in His Son, Jesus Christ. In other words, the way to possess eternal life is to possess God's Son. The question is how can a person have the Son of God?

Man's Problem

Separation From God

On one side of the bridge is God. On the other side are people. Between God and people is a great gap, a division that exists because of our tendency to rebel against God's way and go our own way instead. This is what the Bible calls "sin."

> *"But your iniquities have made a separation between you and God, And your sins have hidden His face from you, so that He does not hear."*
>
> **Isaiah 59:2** (English Standard Version)

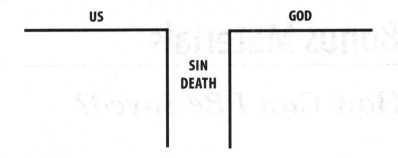

The Uselessness of Our Works

The dilemma that we face is that we want to get to God, but we know we can't just leap over the gap. So we try using human effort to build a bridge until we finally realize that all the human effort in the world will never be enough to get us to the other side.

The Bible teaches that no amount of human goodness, works, morality, or religious activity can gain acceptance with God or get anyone into heaven. We *all* fall short of God's perfect righteousness.

```
         Sinful US                              Holy GOD
  ┌──────────────┐                      ┌──────────────────
  │           ┌──┴────────────┐         │
  │           │ GOOD WORKS    │         │
  │           │ RELIGION      │         │
  │           │ MORALITY      │         │
  │           └──┬────────────┘         │
  │              │                      │
```

After discussing the immoral man, the moral man, and the
religious man in Romans 1:18-3:8, the Apostle Paul declares
that both Jews and Greeks are under sin, that "there is
none righteous, not even one" (Rom. 3:9-10). Added to this
are the following verses from the Bible:

> *"For it is by grace you have been saved, through
> faith—and this not from yourselves, it is the gift of
> God—not by works, so that no one can boast."*
> **Ephesians 2:8-9** (NIV)

> *"He saved us, not because of righteous things we
> had done, but because of His mercy. He saved us
> through the washing of rebirth and renewal by the
> Holy Spirit, whom He poured out on us generously
> through Jesus Christ our Savior, so that, having
> been justified by His grace, we might become heirs
> having the hope of eternal life."*
> **Titus 3:5-7** (NIV)

No amount of human goodness is as good as God. God is
holy and perfect. Because of this, Habakkuk 1:13 tells us
God cannot have fellowship with anyone who does not
have perfect righteousness. In order to be accepted by God,
we must be as good as God is. Before God, we all stand sinful, helpless, and hopeless in ourselves. No amount of good
living will get us to heaven or give us eternal life. What
then is the solution?

God's Solution

Thankfully, God sympathized with our dilemma and because He loves us so much, He intervened so that we can have a way to getting close to Him. His solution was to choose His only Son Jesus Christ to serve as a bridge.

> *"But God demonstrates His own love toward for us in this: while we were still sinners, Christ died for us."*
>
> **Romans 5:8** (NIV)

According to Romans 5:8, God demonstrated His love for us through the death of His Son. Why did Christ have to die for us? Because Scripture declares all men to be sinful. To "sin" means to miss the mark. The Bible declares "all have sinned and fall short of the glory (the perfect holiness) of God" (Rom. 3:23). In other words, our sin separates us from God who is perfect holiness (righteousness and justice) and God must therefore judge sinful man.

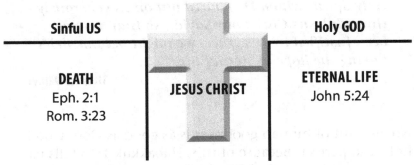

This is the message of the gospel. It's the message of the gift of God's own Son who became man (the God-man), lived a sinless life, died on the cross to become payment for our sin, and was raised from the grave proving both the fact He is God's Son and the value of His death for us as our substitute. Jesus became our *bridge* to God and Eternal Life.

> *"I tell you the truth, whoever hears My word and believes Him who sent Me has eternal life and will not be condemned; he has crossed over from death to life."*
>
> **John 5:24** (NIV)

> *"He was delivered over to death for our sins and was raised to life for our justification."*
>
> **Romans 4:25** (NIV)

> *"God made Him who had no sin to be sin for us, so that in Him we might become the righteousness of God."*
>
> **2 Corinthians 5:21** (NIV)

How Do We Receive God's Son?

Because of what Jesus Christ accomplished for us on the cross, the Bible states "He that has the Son has life." We can receive the Son, Jesus Christ, as our Savior by trusting in the person of Christ and His death for our sins.

> *"Yet to all who received Him, to those who believed in His name, He gave the right to become children of God—"*
>
> **John 1:12** (NIV)

> *"For God so loved the world that He gave His one and only Son, that whoever believes in Him shall not perish but have eternal life. For God did not send His Son into the world to condemn the world, but to save the world through Him. Whoever believes in Him is not condemned, but whoever does not believe stands condemned already because he has not believed in the name of God's one and only Son."*
>
> **John 3:16-18** (NIV)

This means we must each come to God the same way:

1. as a sinner who recognizes his/her sinfulness,
2. realizes no human works can result in salvation, and
3. relies totally on Christ alone by faith alone for our salvation.

If you would like to receive and trust Christ as your personal Savior, you may want to express your faith in Christ by a simple prayer acknowledging your sinfulness, accepting His forgiveness and putting your faith in Christ for your salvation.

Sample Prayer

Dear Lord,

I admit that I am a sinner. I have done things that don't please You. I have lived my life for myself. I am sorry and I repent. I ask You to forgive me of my sins. I believe that You died on the cross for me as a bridge to save me. You did what I could not do for myself. I come to You now and give You my life.

I truly desire to serve You, Lord Jesus. I desire to be led by Your Holy Spirit so I can faithfully follow and obey you. Thank you Jesus for coming into my life and hearing my prayer. I love You Lord, and I thank You that I will spend all eternity with You. I ask all of this in the name of my Lord and Savior, Jesus Christ.

Amen

Adapted from Biblical Studies Press; www.bible.org

Where Does the Holy Spirit Fit In?

Without the Holy Spirit there is a struggle between your soul and body. Your spirit is dead. Without the Holy Spirit your soul/flesh is in control. Before you come to Christ you live from your soul and body. Your spirit is mostly inactive. The Holy Spirit gives you the power and ability to follow God.

> *"I say then: Walk in the Spirit, and you will not fulfill the lust of the flesh."*
>
> **Galatians 5:16** (AKJV)

a. Jesus was filled/ baptized in the Holy Spirit (John 1:32-33) just as you can be filled and empowered by the Holy Spirit.

b. Why be empowered by the Holy Spirit?

✔ He will guide you into all Truth. (John 16:13).

> *"But when He, the Spirit of truth, comes, He will guide you into all truth. He will not speak on His own; He will speak only what He hears, and He will tell you what is yet to come."*
>
> **John 16:13** (NIV)

✔ The Holy Spirit will continue to teach you all things and bring to our remembrance all that God has said through His Word (John 14:26).

> *"But the Counselor, the Holy Spirit, whom the Father will send in My name, will teach you all things and will remind you of everything I have said to you."*
>
> **John 14:26** (NIV)

✔ He will tell whatever He hears from the Father and He will announce to you things that are to come (John 16:13; Examples: Noah in Genesis 6:13-17; Moses in Exodus 7).

✔ He will give you a supernatural prayer language that will speak directly to God (I Corinthians 14:2)

> *"For anyone who speaks in a tongue does not speak to men but to God. Indeed, no one understands him; he utters mysteries with his spirit."*
>
> **1 Corinthians 14:2** (NIV)

The Holy Spirit's roles:
- Convict you of sin (John 16:7-11)
- Guide and Teacher of Truth (John 16:13)
- Counselor and Helper (John 14:16)
- Fruit Producer (Galatians 5:22-23)

c. How do you become filled with the Holy Spirit? Ask! Luke 11:13

> *"If you then, though you are evil, know how to give good gifts to your children, how much more will your Father in heaven give the Holy Spirit to those who ask Him!"*
>
> **Luke 11:13** (NIV)

Prayer: *God help me keep my spirit pure and untangled by my flesh and soul. I want to be led by your Spirit and I ask that you daily fill my spirit with your Holy Spirit. In Jesus Name. Amen.*

> *"The sacrifices of God are a broken spirit; a broken and contrite* [crushed] *heart, O God, You will not despise."*
>
> **Psalm 51:17** (NIV)

Hiding Place Activation

Jesus knows that we sometimes have internal conflicts when we come to Him. He doesn't reject us for that. In fact, His response to a father who cried out and said with tears, "Lord, I believe; help my unbelief" (Mark 9:24), was compassion and deliverance for that man's son. That same Jesus longs to have you experience His deep love and healing. Jesus longs to restore wholeness of your soul, spirit and body so that you can know Him and experience the abundant life (John 10:10).

To know the Father is not just to know facts about Him. It is to intimately know Him personally, to experience Him in your emotions, to be able to fully trust and rely on Him in spirit and to have healing in your body, soul, and spirit. When you experience that wholeness, then you can love the Lord with all of who you are (Matt 22:37).

The Hebrew name "**Emmanuel**" literally means "**God is with us**". ... When the Israelites came to worship the Creator and **Lord** of all, they sought "**Emmanuel**" as they hoped to experience **God's** presence. Isaiah (7:14)

All through Scripture, the Lord communicates truth by using creative word pictures such as Isaiah talks about God gathers the lambs in his arms and carries them close to his heart (Isaiah 40:11). The Psalmist talks about being covered by the wings of God and finding refuge under his feathers (Psalm 91:4). In both cases, the Lord was speaking metaphorically, creating a picture in the reader's mind so that he or she could better comprehend God's protective care.

One unique aspect of this soul healing ministry approach is that Lord leads the session. While I guide you through the healing prayer words, the Lord directs the session. He creates a Hiding Place where you can connect or be with

Him — a refuge where you know Jesus is there, bringing strength, comfort, peace, insight, healing. This step is foundational in the healing of the soul, because you'll be invited to go back to this Hiding Place of safety with Jesus in each lesson.

The Hiding Place exercise is a follows:

* Sit quietly in a comfortable position. Close your eyes the entire time so you're not distracted.

* Take several deep breaths, letting them out slowly. Again breathe in, breathe out.

First, I'm going to pray Scripture over you.

Psalm 31: 2 *So hide all Your beloved ones in the sheltered, secret hiding place before Your face. Overshadow them by Your glory-presence...Tuck them safely away in the tabernacle where You dwell.*

Psalm 9:9 *All who are oppressed may come to You as a shelter in the time of trouble, a perfect hiding place.*

Psalm 36:7 *O God, how extravagant is Your cherishing love! All mankind can find a hiding place under the shadow of Your wings.*

Psalm 17:8 *Protect them from harm; keep an eye on them like You would a child[a] reflected in the twinkling of Your eye. Yes, hide them within the shelter of Your embrace, under Your out-stretched wings.[b]*

Now I want you to pray after me, portions from Psalm 91 changed to first person:
91 *When I sit enthroned / under the shadow of Shaddai, / I am hidden / in the strength of God Most High. He's the hope that holds me / and the Stronghold to shelter me, / the only God for me, / and my great confidence. /He will rescue me / from*

every hidden trap / of the enemy. When I live my life / within the shadow / of God Most High, /our secret hiding place,/ I will always be shielded from harm. For here / is what the Lord / has spoken to me: /"Because you have / delighted in Me/ as My great lover, / I will greatly protect you./ I will set you / in a high place, / safe and secure / before My face. / I will answer / your cry for help / every time you pray, / and you will find / and feel My presence / even in your time / of pressure and trouble./ I will be / your glorious Hero / and give you a feast.

* Begin to whisper words of thanks and praise to the Lord.

* Now, we're going to invite the Holy Spirit to take over your imagination so you can find your Hiding Place. It may be an imaginary place or somewhere you have actually been before that is special, like a cabin, beach, in the woods, or spot by quiet waters.

Say outloud: *Holy Spirit, / I ask You to take over my soul / and purify my imagination. / Let my thoughts,/ be Your thoughts. / My creative mind / is Your creative mind. / I ask you now / to show /or create within my mind /a Hiding Place /where You and I / can meet.*

Write down whatever you see, hear, feel or know.

* Rest there for as long as you like, enjoying all the surroundings. If you experience some dissonance or distraction, ask Holy Spirit to take it away in the name of Jesus.

* Some of you already see or know the Lord is there. If not, when you're ready, invite the Lord to join you in that place. **Say outloud:** *Lord, / I want You / to join me / in my Hiding Place. / Come now Lord /and show me / where You are.*

* You may notice the warmth of His love. Let it soak into your being. If you are allowing Jesus to be there, notice His posture, His eyes, and extended arms. Draw close to Him if you desire.

---

* When ready, tell Jesus how you feel about Him. Then ask how He feels about you. He may respond with words or maybe actions. Either way, experience His acceptance and delight.

* If you are ready to conclude the exercise, simply spend a few moments in thanks and praise.

* Take a few deep breaths, letting them out slowly. Amen

The Hiding Place exercise may take time to develop as a [spiritual] skill. Many believers, accustomed to a more cognitive expression of the Christian life may have never experienced the Lord in this way.

The idea of giving the Lord access to their "creative imagination" might seem like a foreign concept. It is important that the believer practice this spiritual exercise every day. This will be not only a place of peace with the Lord, but it also will be the entree into experiencing the Lord in the healing of past traumatic wounds or trauma.

IF you have problems connecting with God in your Hiding Place:
If you can't see Jesus in your hiding place, you can pray, *"Jesus, open my ears, my eyes and my heart to You. Please help me to be aware of Your presence with me here."*

Or, simply pray: *"Jesus, I need your help. Show me what is getting in the way of me connecting to You. What do I need to do to take the next step forward"* Perhaps playing some worship music that you love may help.

Focus on Jesus and interact with Him. This may be verbal or nonverbal. You can pray, *"Lord, what do you want me to know about You? Jesus, do you have more for me in this situation? Help me to receive everything You have for me here."*
If you've not yet had an experience of connecting with

God in your hiding place, some find it helpful to use positive memories and appreciation for establishing an interactive connection with God. The goal is to find a moment where you felt God's presence. Here are some examples of positive memories:

- Holding one of your children as a newborn baby
- Some other particularly beautiful experience with one of your children
- A favorite family Christmas memory
- Playing with a favorite pet
- An especially positive time with friends
- Some beautiful nature experience
- Connecting with Jesus in the context of a particularly beautiful worship service.

And then observe and describe whatever comes into your awareness.

Ask Jesus, "How do You feel about being with me?" and then observe and describe whatever comes into your awareness.

Another approach is to think of a place where you love to spend time. Invite Jesus to that place. That can be a special Hiding Place for your time with Jesus.

The purpose of spending more time in His presence builds the capacity for you to face your pain and/or trauma and give it to Jesus. This process will happen in every lesson of this transformational journey.

This was created and adapted from several resources including:
Introduction to Heart Sync Model of Healing https://ihouseofhope.com/uploads/3/4/7/5/34755627/what_is_heartsync.pdf

Strong Winds & Crashing Waves by Terry Wardle (pp. 83-85)
A Spirit-led exercise to practice the presence of the Lord https://thecounselingmoment.wordpress.com/2011/01/18/the-safe-place/
Scripture was primarily taken from The Passion Translation

Post Abortive Healing

Please know that many post abortive women (and some men) go through a more in-depth Post Abortion program or Bible Study as healing from an abortion is a journey. I've listed recommended resources from a friend who has been on this journey. She strongly recommends that someone go through these programs either in a one on one setting with a leader or in a group setting with leaders and other post abortive women (or men for a men's group).

Bible Study Curriculum Titles:
Forgiven & Set Free by Linda Cochrane
Surrendering the Secret by Pat Payton
Living in Color by Jenny McDermid

Weekend Retreats:
Deeper Still – www.GoDeeperStill.org
Rachel's Vineyard – www.RachelsVineyard.org

Healing Prayer for Those Who have had an Abortion (to be prayed with the Post Abortive person)
"Lord my God, I cried to You for help, and You healed me."
(Psalm 30:2)

Repeat after Me: *Oh Lord, /I had an abortion/ and the grief and guilt/ I have felt ever since I made that decision / has haunted me. / I feel so ashamed of myself / and riddled with guilt, / by allowing a little life / to be taken in this way.*

My heart is so heavy / and I find that I am not able / to think about anything else / I realize more and more / that it is against You Lord, / that I have sinned / and done this great wrong.

Lord, I feel broken inside / and pray for Your healing and comfort. /You have promised/ to mend the broken-hearted / and to set those that / are captive to guilt and shame free,/ and Lord, /You have promised forgiveness / and restoration / to all who come humbly/ to Your throne of grace / and confess their wrong-doing. /My hope is in You, /for You alone / can restore / the joy of my salvation.

Thank You, / that You are / a forgiving God,/ Your mercies are new every morning /and You have promised / to carry all our guilt and burdens,/ and so I hand this over / to You today. / I ask for the healing and restoration/ that only You can give, / and the grace to forget / what is past / and move on / with You as my guide. / I ask this all in Jesus' name,/ Amen.
Source: https://prayer.knowing-jesus.com/Prayer-for-Abortion

Post Abortive Healing Process and Prayer for Women

"Lord my God, I cried to You for help, and You healed me." (Psalm 30:2)

Begin by praying, *"Jesus, I don't want to be chained any longer by memories of my abortion. Please come and heal me."* Now ask the Holy Spirit to bring up any memories of your abortion: perhaps of the day you discovered you were pregnant; the reactions of the child's father or your parents; the feeling of abandonment; the dilemma of making the decision to go to the abortion clinic; the actual procedure; the days following the abortion; or any other memories or flashbacks you find troubling. Write what comes back to you here:

_____

_____

_____

Do the Divine Exchange. As a memory comes back to your mind, ask Jesus to come into the memory. Then wait, and expect to see Jesus in the midst of your memory. Now simply allow yourself to feel the pain and then give it to Jesus. What is Jesus doing now? Is He reaching out his hands to you, hugging you, or maybe drying your tears? Say to Jesus, *"Please heal this memory so that it no longer keeps me chained."* Finally, listen to what Jesus says to you and write it down.

_____

_____

_____

Receive His peace. Jesus bore the pain of this memory when He died on the cross. Say, *Thank you risen Lord for You have healed my memory."* Don't rush. Let the tears flow. Crying is healing. Psalm 126:5 says "May those who sow in tears reap with shouts of joy".

And don't worry if you can't see Jesus in your mind or hear him say anything. Not everyone does. But trust that Jesus is with you. He sees you, and he hears the cries of your heart. Jesus is holding you. He's crying with you. Jesus is feeling your distress. He's receiving all your pain upon himself. Jesus is healing you.

Healing of Grief
Ask the Holy Spirit to help you identify your losses. Then write them down here.

_____

_____

_____

Talk to Jesus about your grief and your pain. Jesus is the Healer. He is listening and is right there with you. When you are ready, say, *"Jesus, I give you my grief and my pain. Thank you for receiving all my pain and grief."*

Turn to Jesus and pray, *"Jesus, just like the woman in the Scriptures, I reach out my hand to touch the hem of your cloak. I ask for the healing power that flows from your cross and resurrection to flow through my body and to heal me of these physical or emotional conditions related to my abortion* (name them).*"*

Take a moment to hear Jesus say, "I am always with you, _____(insert name)_____." If you have any memories of people letting you down, lying to you, or just not being there for you—especially regarding your abortion—stop for a few minutes. Ask Jesus to forgive you for any anger or resentment you still feel. Then follow the steps in the previous reflection for the healing of memories because Jesus is your Healer.

Pray now with great expectancy, *"Holy Spirit, come and baptize me with the fire of your love."* Don't rush. Sit for five or ten minutes, and allow the Holy Spirit to minister to you in whatever way He chooses. Perhaps you will experience a special sense of His presence. Perhaps a word or thought you know is not your own or a few words from a Scripture verse will pop into your head. Or perhaps you will see a picture in your mind. Whatever it is, it will be something very personal, just for you! Write about this time of prayer in your journal.

_____

_____

_____

Holy Spirit wants to replace them with these Truths. Please repeat them after me:
- My child is a beloved son/daughter of God (Psalm 139).
- My child is in heaven – I am his/her mother (Genesis 1:27).
- I am forgiven for aborting my child. My sin is redeemed (Colossians 1:13-14).
- I can, with confidence, entrust my child to the Lord (Luke 12:7).

Here's one more thought about your child: why not choose a name for your child? Remember! You hope to be living with your child in the presence of the Lord for all of eternity.

Say to your child, "I am naming you _____ !" Enjoy this time thinking about your child. Receive all the inner healing that the Holy Spirit is doing in your life right now. Remember this is a journey and there are layers of pain for Jesus to heal. Holy Spirit loves you and wants to fill you with his awesome transforming power. What you believe, you will receive!

Healing Process and Prayer for Men Who Aborted a Child
"Lord my God, I cried to You for help, and You healed me." (Psalm 30:2)

Begin by praying, *"Jesus, I don't want to be chained any longer by memories of my abortion decision. Please come and heal me."* Now ask the Holy Spirit to bring up any memories of the abortion decision: perhaps of the day you discovered your partner was pregnant; the reactions of your partner or your parents; feelings of resentment or anger; the dilemma of making the decision to go to the abortion clinic; the day of the actual procedure; the days following the abortion; or any other memories or flashbacks you find troubling.

As a memory comes back to your mind, ask Jesus to come into the memory. Then wait, and expect to see Jesus in the midst of your memory. Now simply allow yourself to feel the pain. What is Jesus doing now? Is he reaching out his hands to you, hugging you, or maybe drying your tears? Say to Jesus, *"Please heal this memory so that it no longer keeps me chained."*

Finally, listen to what Jesus says to you. Perhaps he is saying, "I was there all the time with you. Receive my peace. I bore the pain of this memory when I died on the cross. I'm your risen Lord. I have healed your memory." Don't rush.

If there are tears, allow them to flow. Crying is healing. *"May those who sow in tears reap with shouts of joy"* (Psalm 126:5).

Ask Holy Spirit to help you identify your losses. Then write them down:

_____

_____

_____

What is grief? Grief is a deep sorrow and sadness. Grief is painful and emotionally exhausting. Grief can leave a person feeling empty and numb. And grief is normal after a loss. So give yourself permission to grieve the loss or losses you've identified. Don't be afraid to feel the grief and the pain of your losses. Your grief is real. And your pain is real. But if you allow yourself to heal, the pain you are feeling now will diminish over time.

Do the Divine Exchange: Talk to Jesus about your grief and your pain. Jesus is the Healer. He is listening and is right there with you. When you are ready, say, *"Jesus, I give you my grief and my pain. Please take it all."*

Spend some time in prayer with your eyes closed, and ask God your Father to come in and heal this wound of shame in your heart. Identify the pain in your heart or wherever you feel it, and ask God to place His healing hand upon you, and to come in and heal that pain. He desires to do this. You may want to repeat this prayer during your journey to healing as God your Father heals your wound.

From: https://waupartners.org/resources/article/after_abortion_forgiveness_healing_and_hope

Protection Prayers Before and After Ministering Soul Healing

Morning Prayer by Erin Lamb* This prayer has been instrumental in protecting me spiritually from the enemy's attacks. When you are used to heal others, the enemy really does not want you to do this. I pray this every morning and certainly before going out to minister.

From 2 Corinthians 10:3-5 I do live in the world. But I don't fight my battles the way the people of the world do. The weapons I fight with are not the weapons the world uses. In fact, it is just the opposite. My weapons have the power of God to destroy the camps of the enemy. I destroy every claim and every reason that keeps people from knowing God. I keep every thought under control in order to make it obey Christ. (NIRV)

In the name of Jesus, I take authority over this day. I bind all accidents, sickness, death, and destruction-all works of darkness. I plead the blood of Jesus over me and my entire metron (sphere of influence/authority). I proclaim Psalm 91 over me. I cancel demonic assignments against those under my authority, my family, my business, over those I pray for.

Today will be a great day! I am empowered by God to win and do incredible things. His mercy is new each morning. I am MORE than a conqueror through Christ who gives me His strength. God's JOY is my strength and I stand in the resurrected power of Jesus.

I bind demons operating in people around me from manifesting and negatively influencing them or me. I walk in supernatural health, wealth, wisdom, and prosperity!! I carry a double portion anointing. I have the healer in me! I have the deliverer in me. The power of God is in me and upon me!! I walk in the supernatural power of God. The fire of God is in me. Greater is He who is in me, than in the world. The devil and no demon is greater than the God in me!

I pray for the sick and they recover! I pray for the oppressed and they are delivered! I decree life over dead things and they come alive according to His will. Sickness has no place in me. Defeat has no place in me. Debt has no place in me. The devil has no authority over my destiny!! I am the HEAD and not the TAIL!! Blessings overtake me. God's goodness and mercy follow me.

I am a world changer and HIStory maker for Jesus. Where I go, God's love and power are put on display. God sets up divine appointments for me to bless others. I believe all the promises of God are YES and AMEN for me. My prayers aligned with heaven are answered. As I walk with Jesus miracles happen. Portals to heaven are opened. I live under an open heaven!!

I am blessed as I unite my heart to God and abide in Jesus. As I abide, I bear good fruit! In Jesus name I walk by faith!! My mustard seed faith moves mountains. Mountains in the way of God's plans MOVE by the power of God!

Prayer adapted from a prayer from Erin Lamb. https:// ithoughtiknewwhatlovewas.com/ https://www.empowered-free.com/

Midnight Prayers by Dr. D.K. Olukoya
Make These Declarations Out Loud and Pray Them One by One

I use this comprehensive prayer after ministering to others or if I'm feeling attacked in any way. This is also helpful if you are experiencing bad dreams.

I put on the full armor of God now in Jesus name according to Ephesians 6:10-18:
- The belt of truth
- The breastplate of righteousness
- The helmet of salvation
- The shoes of peace
- The shield of faith
- The sword of the Spirit

I position myself in the spiritual realm and call upon the Lord of Hosts and His Angels of Deliverance to minister on my behalf in Jesus name.

I soak my spirit soul and body in the blood of Jesus Christ and declare that this is the day of my great deliverance, healing and breakthrough by fire and by force in Jesus name.

I close every door by the blood of Jesus that was opened by me knowingly or unknowingly that might hinder my prayers. I close it now in Jesus name.

Midnight Declarations

1. **Now touch your head and repeat this several times (x 12) until you can feel a release:** Jesus Christ of Nazareth baptize me now with the Holy Ghost and fire in Jesus name.

2. Every strange spirit attacking my life; be destroyed now by fire in Jesus name.

---

3. Generational bondages, curses and the strongman of my father's house let me loose now by fire in Jesus name.

4. **Touch your naval/stomach as you pray this prayer:** I cut and disconnect myself from any spiritual cord that is connecting me to demonic foundations, marine* altars and human spirits; I cut it now with the sword of the Spirit by fire in Jesus name.

5. I break the spirit of poverty and command every blessing that belongs to me; to be vomited now by the marine serpent in Jesus name.

6. I disconnect myself from marine altars and demonic dreams; I disconnect my life from their influence in Jesus name.

7. I destroy the spiritual wife/husband assigned to destroy my life; I arrest them now by fire in Jesus name.
8. I renounce every involvement in the demonic kingdom that I have ever entered into.

9. I destroy every contract binding my destiny in Jesus name.

10. I call down fire upon every assembly of the kingdom of darkness assigned to destroy me. Let fire consume them now in Jesus name.

11. I receive total deliverance from demonic covenants.

12. I shall live and not die to proclaim the glory of God.

13. Every evil monitoring spirit, monitoring my progress; be arrested now by fire in Jesus name.

14. Enemies of progress against my success be paralyzed by fire and die in Jesus name.

Healing Your Soul

15. I take all my riches, gifts and blessings held up by the serpent in Jesus name.

16. I take my prayer life back in Jesus name.

17. Holy Ghost fire, purge my life completely in Jesus name.

18. I claim my complete deliverance in the name of Jesus Christ from all domestic demonic covenants in Jesus mighty name.

19. **Lay your hand on your head and another on your stomach and begin to pray this:** Holy Ghost fire, burn from the top of my head to the sole of my feet now in Jesus name.

20. I accelerate from bondage to freedom in every area of my life in Jesus name.

21. I command every evil plantation in my life: Come out now by fire with all your roots in Jesus mighty name.

22. Every evil stranger in my body I cast you out now by fire in Jesus mighty name.

23. **Begin to touch your head, neck, chest, stomach, etc. and keep repeating this prayer:** I take all authority and legal rights back in Jesus mighty name.

Give thanks and have a goodnight's rest!

*Marine spirits/altars are one of the principality groups over America. These spirits include Jezebel, Leviathan, python, lizard spirits, seduction, homosexuality, child molestation, porn, human trafficking, lust, etc. Resource Book: *Powerful Prayers Against Marine Spirits* by Dr. Olusola Cooker. I also recommend Breakthrough Tablets for Healing and Wholeness (7 day program) from: *The Jehu Prayers*, Dr. D.K. Olukoya. 2012 in Yaba, Lagos (Nigeria). Dr. DKO has numerous YouTube videos as well.

Free Masonry Prayer of Renunciation

I strongly encourage you to read through this prayer as instructed below. It's the most comprehensive Free Masonry Prayer of Renunciation that I've found and it's extremely effective in cutting off the many generational curses that come from freemasonry. In addition to being the world's oldest fraternal organization, Freemasonry is also the world's largest such organization, boasting an estimated worldwide membership of some 6 million people, according to a report by the BBC. Therefore, you may have freemasonry in your lineage. Regardless of your ancestry, it doesn't hurt to read this.

It is best to pray this aloud with a Christian witness present. We suggest a brief pause following each paragraph to allow the Holy Spirit to show any related issues which may require attention.

A significant number of people also reported having experienced physical and spiritual healings as diverse as long-term headaches and epilepsy as the result of praying through this prayer. Christian counsellors and pastors in many countries have been using this prayer in counselling situations and seminars for several years, with real and significant results.

Some language could be described as 'quaint Old English' and are the real terms used in the Masonic ritual. The legal renunciation opens the way for spiritual, emotional and physical healing to take place.

There are differences between British Commonwealth Masonry and American & Prince Hall Masonry in the higher degrees. Degrees unique to Americans are marked with this sign "*" at the commencement of each paragraph. Those of British Commonwealth descent shouldn't need to pray through those paragraphs.

The Prayer of Release

Father God, creator of heaven and earth, I come to you
in the name of Jesus Christ your Son. I come as a sinner
seeking forgiveness and cleansing from all sins committed
against you, and others made in your image. I honour my
earthly father and mother and all of my ancestors of flesh
and blood, and of the spirit by adoption and godparents,
but I utterly turn away from and renounce all their sins. I
forgive all my ancestors for the effects of their sins on me
and my children. I confess and renounce all of my own
sins, known and unknown. I renounce and rebuke Satan
and every spiritual power of his affecting me and my family, in the name of Jesus Christ.

True Holy Creator God, in the name of the True Lord Jesus Christ, in accordance with Jude 8-10; Psalm 82:1 and
2 Chronicles 18, I request you to move aside all Celestial
Beings, including Principalities, Powers and Rulers, and to
forbid them to harass, intimidate or retaliate against me
and all participants in this ministry today.

I also ask that you prevent and forbid these beings, of
whatever rank, from sending any level of spiritual evil as
retaliation against any of those here, or our families, our
ministries, or possessions.

I renounce and annul every covenant made with Death by
my ancestors or myself, including every agreement made
with Sheol, and I renounce the refuge of lies and false-
hoods which have been hidden behind.

In the name of the Lord Jesus Christ, I renounce and forsake all involvement in Freemasonry or any other lodge,
craft or occultism by my ancestors and myself. I also renounce and break the code of silence enforced by Freemasonry and the Occult on my family and myself. I renounce
and repent of all pride and arrogance which opened the
door for the slavery and bondage of Freemasonry to afflict

my family and me. I now shut every door of witchcraft and deception operating in my life and seal it closed with the blood of the Lord Jesus Christ. I renounce every covenant, every blood covenant and every alliance with Freemasonry or the spiritual powers behind it made by my family or me.

In the name of Jesus Christ, I rebuke, renounce and bind Witchcraft, the principal spirit behind Freemasonry, and I renounce and rebuke Baphomet, the Spirit of Antichrist and the spirits of Death, and Deception.

I renounce and rebuke the Spirit of Fides, the Roman goddess of Fidelity that seeks to hold all Masonic and occultic participants and their descendants in bondage, and I ask the One True Holy Creator God to give me the gift of Faith to believe in the True Lord Jesus Christ as described in the Word of God.

I also renounce and rebuke the Spirit of Prostitution which the Word of God says has led members of Masonic and other Occultic organisations astray, and caused them to become unfaithful to the One True and Holy God. I now choose to return and become faithful to the God of the Bible, the God of Abraham, Isaac and Jacob, the Father of Jesus Christ, who I now declare is my Lord and Saviour.

I renounce the insecurity, the love of position and power, the love of money, avarice or greed, and the pride which would have led my ancestors into Masonry. I renounce all the fears which held them in Masonry, especially the fears of death, fears of men, and fears of trusting, in the name of Jesus Christ.

I renounce every position held in the lodge by any of my ancestors or myself, including "Master," "Worshipful Master," or any other occultic title. I renounce the calling of any man "Master," for Jesus Christ is my only master and Lord, and He forbids anyone else having that title. I renounce the entrapping of others into Masonry, and observing the helplessness of others during the rituals. I renounce the effects of Masonry passed on to me through any female ancestor who felt distrusted and rejected by her husband as he entered and attended any lodge and refused to tell her of his secret activities. I also renounce all obligations, oaths and curses enacted by every female member of my family through any direct membership of all Women's Orders of Freemasonry, the Order of the Eastern Star, or any other Masonic or occultic organisation.

All participants should now be invited to sincerely carry out in faith the following actions:
1. Symbolically remove the blindfold (hoodwink) and give it to the Lord for disposal;
2. In the same way, symbolically remove the veil of mourning, to make way to receive the Joy of the Lord:
3. Symbolically cut and remove the noose from around the neck, gather it up with the cabletow running down the body and give it all to the Lord for His disposal;
4. Renounce the false Freemasonry marriage covenant, removing from the 4th finger of the right hand the ring of this false marriage covenant, giving it to the Lord to dispose of it;
5. Symbolically remove the chains and bondages of Freemasonry from your body;
6. Symbolically remove all Freemasonry regalia, including collars, gauntlets and armour, especially the Apron with its snake clasp, to make way for the Belt of Truth;
7. Remove the slipshod slippers, to make way for the shoes of the Gospel of Peace;
8. Symbolically remove the ball and chain from the ankles.
9. Invite participants to repent of and seek forgiveness for having walked on all unholy ground, including Freemasonry lodges and temples, including any Mormon or any other occultic/Masonic organisations.
10. Proclaim that Satan and his demons no longer have any legal rights to mislead and manipulate the person seeking help.

33rd & Supreme Degree

In the name of Jesus Christ I renounce the oaths taken and the curses and iniquities involved in the supreme Thirty-Third Degree of Freemasonry, the Grand Sovereign Inspector General. I renounce the secret passwords, DEMOLAY-HIRUM ABIFF, FREDERICK OF PRUSSIA, MICHA, MACHA, BEALIM, and ADONAI, and all their occultic and Masonic meanings. I renounce all of the obligations of every Masonic degree, and all penalties invoked.

I renounce and utterly forsake The Great Architect Of The Universe, who is revealed in the this degree as Lucifer, and his false claim to be the universal fatherhood of God. I reject the Masonic view of deity because it does not square with the revelation of the One True and Holy Creator God of the Bible.

I renounce the cable-tow around the neck. I renounce the death wish that the wine drunk from a human skull should turn to poison and the skeleton whose cold arms are invited if the oath of this degree is violated. I renounce the three infamous assassins of their grand master, law, property and religion, and the greed and witchcraft involved in the attempt to manipulate and control the rest of mankind.

In the name of God the Father, Jesus Christ the Son, and the Holy Spirit, I renounce and break the curses and iniquities involved in the idolatry, blasphemy, secrecy and deception of Freemasonry at every level, and I appropriate the Blood of Jesus Christ to cleanse all the consequences of these from my life. I now revoke all previous consent given by any of my ancestors or myself to be deceived.

Blue Lodge

In the name of Jesus Christ I renounce the oaths taken and the curses and iniquities involved in the First or Entered Apprentice Degree, especially their effects on the throat and tongue. I renounce the Hoodwink blindfold and its effects on spirit, emotions and eyes, including all confusion, fear of the dark, fear of the light, and fear of sudden noises. I renounce the blinding of spiritual truth, the darkness of the soul, the false imagination, condescension and the spirit of poverty caused by the ritual of this degree. I also renounce the usurping of the marriage covenant by the removal of the wedding ring. I renounce the secret word, BOAZ, and it's Masonic meaning. I renounce the serpent clasp on the apron, and the spirit of Python which it brought to squeeze the spiritual life out of me.

I renounce the ancient pagan teaching from Babylon and Egypt and the symbolism of the First Tracing Board. I renounce the mixing and mingling of truth and error, the mythology, fabrications and lies taught as truth, and the dishonesty by leaders as to the true understanding of the ritual, and the blasphemy of this degree of Freemasonry.

I renounce the breaking of five of God's Ten Commandments during participation in the rituals of the Blue Lodge degrees. I renounce the presentation to every compass direction, for all the Earth is the Lord's, and everything in it. I renounce the cabletow noose around the neck, the fear of choking and also every spirit causing asthma, hayfever, emphysema or any other breathing difficulty. I renounce the ritual dagger, or the compass point, sword or spear held against the breast, the fear of death by stabbing pain, and the fear of heart attack from this degree, and the absolute secrecy demanded under a witchcraft oath and sealed by kissing the Volume of the Sacred Law. I also renounce kneeling to the false deity known as the Great Architect of the Universe, and humbly ask the One True God to forgive me for this idolatry, in the name of Jesus Christ.

I renounce the pride of proven character and good standing required prior to joining Freemasonry, and the resulting self-righteousness of being good enough to stand before God without the need of a saviour. I now pray for healing of... (throat, vocal cords, nasal passages, sinus, bronchial tubes etc.) for healing of the speech area, and the release of the Word of God to me and through me and my family.

Second or Fellow Craft Degree of Masonry

In the name of Jesus Christ I renounce the oaths taken and the curses and iniquities involved in the Second or Fellow Craft Degree of Masonry, especially the curses on the heart and chest. I renounce the secret words SHIBBOLETH and JACHIN, and all their Masonic meaning. I renounce the ancient pagan teaching and symbolism of the Second Tracing Board. I renounce the Sign of Reverence to the Generative Principle. I cut off emotional hardness, apathy, indifference, unbelief, and deep anger from me and my family. In the name of Jesus' Christ I pray for the healing of ...(the chest/lung/heart area) and also for the healing of my emotions, and ask to be made sensitive to the Holy Spirit of God.

Third or Master Mason Degree

In the name of Jesus Christ I renounce the oaths taken and the curses and iniquities involved in the Third or Master Mason Degree, especially the curses on the stomach and womb area. I renounce the secret words TUBAL CAIN and MAHA BONE, and all their Masonic meaning. I renounce the ancient pagan teaching and symbolism of the Third Tracing Board used in the ritual. I renounce the Spirit of Death from the blows to the head enacted as ritual murder, the fear of death, false martyrdom, fear of violent gang attack, assault, or rape, and the helplessness of this degree. I renounce the falling into the coffin or stretcher involved in the ritual of murder.

In the name of Jesus Christ I renounce Hiram Abiff, the false saviour of Freemasons revealed in this degree. I renounce the false resurrection of this degree, because only Jesus Christ is the Resurrection and the Life!

I renounce the pagan ritual of the "Point within a Circle" with all its bondages and phallus worship. I renounce the symbol "G" and its veiled pagan symbolism and bondages. I renounce the occultic mysticism of the black and white mosaic chequered floor with the tessellated boarder and five-pointed blazing star.

I renounce the All-Seeing Third Eye of Freemasonry or Horus in the forehead and its pagan and occult symbolism. I rebuke and reject every spirit of divination which allowed this occult ability to operate. Action: Put your hand over your forehead.) I now close that Third eye and all occult ability to see into the spiritual realm, in the name of the Lord Jesus Christ, and put my trust in the Holy Spirit sent by Jesus Christ for all I need to know on spiritual matters. I renounce all false communions taken, all mockery of the redemptive work of Jesus Christ on the cross of Calvary, all unbelief, confusion and depression. I renounce and forsake the lie of Freemasonry that man is not sinful, but merely imperfect, and so can redeem himself through good works. I rejoice that the Bible states that I cannot do a single thing to earn my salvation, but that I can only be saved by grace through faith in Jesus Christ and what He accomplished on the Cross of Calvary.

I renounce all fear of insanity, anguish, death wishes, suicide and death in the name of Jesus Christ. Death was conquered by Jesus Christ, and He alone holds the keys of death and hell, and I rejoice that He holds my life in His hands now. He came to give me life abundantly and eternally, and I believe His promises.

I renounce all anger, hatred, murderous thoughts, revenge, retaliation, spiritual apathy, false religion, all unbelief, especially unbelief in the Holy Bible as God's Word, and all compromise of God's Word. I renounce all spiritual searching into false religions, and all striving to please God. I rest in the knowledge that I have found my Lord and Saviour Jesus Christ, and that He has found me.

In the name of Jesus Christ I pray for the healing of... (the stomach, gall bladder, womb, liver, and any other organs of my body affected by Masonry), and I ask for a release of compassion and understanding for me and my family.

York Rite
I renounce and forsake the oaths taken and the curses and iniquities involved in the York Rite Degrees of Masonry. I renounce the Mark Lodge, and the mark in the form of squares and angles which marks the person for life. I also reject the jewel or occult talisman which may have been made from this mark sign and worn at lodge meetings; <br. the Mark Master Degree with its secret word JOPPA, and its penalty of having the right ear smote off and the curse of permanent deafness, as well as the right hand being chopped off for being an imposter.

I also renounce and forsake the oaths taken and the curses and iniquities involved in the other York Rite Degrees, including Past Master, with the penalty of having my tongue split from tip to root; <br. and of the Most Excellent Master Degree, in which the penalty is to have my breast torn open and my heart and vital organs removed and exposed to rot on the dung hill.

Holy Royal Arch Degree
In the name of Jesus Christ, I renounce and forsake the oaths taken and the curses and iniquities involved in the Holy Royal Arch Degree especially the oath regarding the removal of the head from the body and the exposing of the brains to the hot sun. I renounce the false secret name of God, JAHBULON, and declare total rejection of all worship of the false pagan gods, Bul or Baal, and On or Osiris. I also renounce the password, AMMI RUHAMAH and all it's Masonic meaning. I renounce the false communion or Eucharist taken in this degree, and all the mockery, scepticism and unbelief about the redemptive work of Jesus Christ on the cross of Calvary. I cut off all these curses and their effects on me and my family in the name of Jesus Christ, and I pray for… (healing of the brain, the mind etc.)

I renounce and forsake the oaths taken and the curses and iniquities involved in the Royal Master Degree of the York Rite; the Select Master Degree with its penalty to have my hands chopped off to the stumps, to have my eyes plucked out from their sockets, and to have my body quartered and thrown among the rubbish of the Temple.

I renounce and forsake the oaths taken and the curses and iniquities involved in the Super Excellent Master Degree along with the penalty of having my thumbs cut off, my eyes put out, my body bound in fetters and brass, and conveyed captive to a strange land; and also of the Knights or Illustrious Order of the Red Cross, along with the penalty of having my house torn down and my being hanged on the exposed timbers.

I renounce the Knights Templar Degree and the secret words of KEB RAIOTH, and also Knights of Malta Degree and the secret words MAHER-SHALAL-HASH-BAZ.

I renounce the vows taken on a human skull, the crossed swords, and the curse and death wish of Judas of having the head cut off and placed on top of a church spire. I renounce the unholy communion and especially of drinking from a human skull in many Rites.

Ancient & Accepted or Scottish Rite
(Only the 18th, 30th, 31st 32nd & 33rd degree are operated in British Commonwealth countries.)
*** * I renounce the oaths taken and the curses, iniquities and penalties involved in the American and Grand Orient Lodges, including of the Secret Master Degree, its secret passwords of ADONAI and ZIZA, and their occult meanings. I reject and renounce the worship of the pagan sun god as the Great Source of Light, and the crowning with laurel – sacred to Apollo, and the sign of secrecy in obedience to Horus;

*** of the Perfect Master Degree, its secret password of MAH-HAH-BONE, and its penalty of being smitten to the Earth with a setting maul;

*** * of the Intimate Secretary Degree, its secret passwords of YEVA and JOABERT, and its penalties of having my body dissected, and of having my vital organs cut into pieces and thrown to the beasts of the field, and of the use of the nine-pointed star from the Kabbala and the worship of Phallic energy;

*** of the Provost and Judge Degree, its secret password of HIRUM-TITO-CIVI-KY, and the penalty of having my nose cut off;

*** of the Intendant of the Building Degree, of its secret password AKAR-JAI-JAH, and the penalty of having my eyes put out, my body cut in two and exposing my bowels;

*** of the Elected Knights of the Nine Degree, its secret password NEKAM NAKAH, and its penalty of having my head cut off and stuck on the highest pole in the East;

*** of the Illustrious Elect of Fifteen Degree, with its secret password ELIGNAM, and its penalties of having my body opened perpendicularly and horizontally, the entrails exposed to the air for eight hours so that flies may prey on them, and for my head to be cut off and placed on a high pinnacle;

*** of the Sublime Knights elect of the Twelve Degree, its secret password STOLKIN-ADONAI, and its penalty of having my hand cut in twain;

*** of the Grand Master Architect Degree, its secret password RAB-BANAIM, and its penalties;

*** * of the Knight of the Ninth Arch of Solomon or Enoch Degree, its secret password JEHOVAH, it's blasphemous use, its penalty of having my body given to the beasts of the forest as prey, and I also renounce the revelations from the Kabbala in this and subsequent degrees;

Healing Your Soul

*** * of the Grand Elect, Perfect and Sublime Mason or Elu Degree, its secret password MARAH-MAUR-ABREK and IHUH, the penalty of having my body cut open and my bowels given to vultures for food, and I reject the Great Unknowable deity of this degree;

Council of Princes of Jerusalem
*** of the Knights of the East Degree, its secret password RAPH-O-DOM, and its penalties;

*** of the Prince of Jerusalem Degree, its secret password TEBET-ADAR, and its penalty of being stripped naked and having my heart pierced with a ritual dagger;

Chapter of the Rose Croix
*** * of the Knight of the East and West Degree, its secret password ABADDON, and its penalty of incurring the severe wrath of the Almighty Creator of Heaven and Earth. I also reject the Tetractys and its representation of the Sephiroth from the Kabbala and its false tree of life. I also reject the false anointing with oil and the proclamation that anyone so anointed is now worthy to open the Book of Seven Seals, because only the Lord Jesus Christ is worthy;

18th Degree
I renounce the oaths taken and the curses, iniquities and penalties involved in the Eighteenth Degree of Freemasonry, the Most Wise Sovereign Knight of the Pelican and the Eagle and Sovereign Prince Rose Croix of Heredom. I renounce and reject the false Jesus revealed in this degree because He doesn't point to the light or the truth since the True Lord Jesus Christ is the Light of the World and the Truth. I renounce and reject the Pelican witchcraft spirit, as well as the occultic influence of the Rosicrucians and the Kabbala in this degree.

I renounce the claim that the death of Jesus Christ was a "dire calamity," and also the deliberate mockery and twisting of the Christian doctrine of the Atonement. I renounce the blasphemy and rejection of the deity of Jesus Christ, and the secret words IGNE NATURA RENOVATUR INTEGRA and its burning. I renounce the mockery of the communion taken in this degree, including a biscuit, salt and white wine.

Council of Kadosh
*** I renounce the inappropriate use of the title "Kadosh" used in these council degrees because it means "Holy" and it is here used in a unholy way.

I renounce the oaths taken and the curses, iniquities and penalties involved in the Grand Pontiff Degree, its secret password EMMANUEL, and its penalties;

*** * of the Grand Master of Symbolic Lodges or Ad Vitum Degree, its secret passwords JEKSON and STOLKIN, and the penalties invoked, and I also reject the pagan Phoenecian and Hindu deities revealed in this degree;

*** * of the Patriarch Noachite or Prussian Knight Degree, its secret password PELEG, and its penalties;

*** * of the Knight of the Royal Axe or Prince of Libanus Degree, its secret password NOAH-BEZALEEL-SODONIAS, and its penalties;

*** * of the Chief of the Tabernacle Degree, its secret password URIEL-JEHOVAH, and its penalty that I agree the Earth should open up and engulf me up to my neck so I perish, and I also reject the false title of becoming a "Son of Light" in this degree;

*** * of the Prince of the Tabernacle Degree, and its penalty to be stoned to death and have my body left above ground to rot. I also reject the claimed revelation of the mysteries of the Hebrew faith from the Kabbala, and the occultic and pagan Egyptian, Hindu, Mithraic, Dionysian and Orphic mysteries revealed and worshipped in this degree;

*** * of the Knight of the Brazen Serpent Degree, its secret password MOSES-JOHANNES, and its penalty to have my heart eaten by venomous serpents. I also reject the claimed revelation of the mysteries of the Islamic faith, I reject the insulting misquotations from the Koran, and the gift of a white turban in this degree;

*** * of the Prince of Mercy Degree, its secret password GOMEL, JEHOVAH-JACHIN, and its penalty of condemnation and spite by the entire universe. I also reject the claimed revelation of the mysteries of the Christian religion because there are no such mysteries. I reject the Druid trinity of Odin, Frea and Thor revealed in this degree. I also reject the false baptism claimed for the purification of my soul to allow my soul to rejoin the universal soul of Buddhism, as taught in this degree;

*** * of the Knight Commander of the Temple Degree, its secret password SOLOMON, and its penalty of receiving the severest wrath of Almighty God inflicted upon me. I also reject the claimed revelation of the mysteries of Numerology, Astrology and Alchemy and other occult sciences taught in this degree;

*** * of the Knight Commander of the Sun, or Prince Adept Degree, its secret password STIBIUM, and its penalties of having my tongue thrust through with a red-hot iron, of my eyes being plucked out, of my senses of smelling and hearing being removed, of having my hands cut off and in that condition to be left for voracious animals to devour me, or executed by lightning from heaven;

*** * of the Grand Scottish Knight of Saint Andrew or Patriarch of the Crusades Degree, its secret password NEKA-MAH-FURLAC, and its penalties;

Thirtieth Degree

I renounce the oaths taken and the curses and iniquities involved in the Thirtieth Degree of Masonry, the Grand Knight Kadosh and Knight of the Black and White Eagle. I renounce the secret passwords, STIBIUM ALKABAR, PHA-RASH-KOH and all they mean.

Sublime Princes of The Royal Secret
Thirty-First Degree of Masonry

I renounce the oaths taken and the curses and iniquities involved in the Thirty-First Degree of Masonry, the Grand Inspector Inquisitor Commander. I renounce all the gods and goddesses of Egypt which are honoured in this degree, including Anubis with the jackel's head, Osiris the Sun god, Isis the sister and wife of Osiris and also the moon goddess. I renounce the Soul of Cheres, the false symbol of immortality, the Chamber of the dead and the false teaching of reincarnation.

Thirty-Second Degree of Masonry

I renounce the oaths taken and the curses and iniquities involved in the Thirty-Second Degree of Masonry, the Sublime Prince of the Royal Secret. I renounce the secret passwords, PHAAL/PHARASH-KOL and all they mean. I renounce Masonry's false trinitarian deity AUM, and its parts; Brahma the creator, Vishnu the preserver and Shiva the destroyer. I renounce the deity of AHURA-MAZDA, the claimed spirit or source of all light, and the worship with fire, which is an abomination to God, and also the drinking from a human skull in many Rites.

Shriners (Applies only in North America)

*** I renounce the oaths taken and the curses, iniquities and penalties involved in the Ancient Arabic Order of the Nobles of the Mystic Shrine. I renounce the piercing of the eyeballs with a three-edged blade, the flaying of the feet, the madness, and the worship of the false god Allah as the god of our fathers. I renounce the hoodwink, the mock hanging, the mock beheading, the mock drinking of the blood of the victim, the mock dog urinating on the initiate, and the offering of urine as a commemoration.

All Other Degrees
I renounce all the other oaths taken, the rituals of every other degree and the curses and iniquities invoked. These include the Acacia, Allied Degrees, The Red Cross of Constantine, the Order of the Secret Monitor, and the Masonic Royal Order of Scotland.

I renounce all other lodges and secret societies including Prince Hall Freemasonry, Grand Orient Lodges, Mormonism, the Ancient Toltec Rite, The Order of Amaranth, the Royal Order of Jesters, the Manchester Unity Order of Oddfellows and its womens' Order of Rebekah lodges, the Royal Antediluvian Order of Buffaloes, Druids, Foresters, the Loyal Order of Orange, including the Purple and Black Lodges within it, Elks, Moose and Eagles Lodges, the Ku Klux Klan, The Grange, the Woodmen of the World, Riders of the Red Robe, the Knights of Pythias, the Order of the Builders, The Rite of Memphiz and Mitzraim, Ordo Templi Orientis (OTO), Aleister Crowley's Palladium Masonry, the Order of the Golden Key, the Order of Desoms, the Mystic Order of the Veiled Prophets of the Enchanted Realm, the women's Orders of the Eastern Star, of the Ladies Oriental Shrine, and of the White Shrine of Jerusalem, the girls' order of the Daughters of the Eastern Star, the International Orders of Job's Daughters, and of the Rainbow, the boys' Order of De Molay, and the Order of the Constellation of Junior Stars, and every university or college Fraternity or Sorority with Greek and Masonic connections, and their effects on me and all my family.

Lord Jesus, because you want me to be totally free from all occult bondages, I will burn all objects in my possession which connect me with all lodges and occultic organisations, including Masonry, Witchcraft, the Occult and Mormonism, and all regalia, aprons, books of rituals, rings and other jewellery. I renounce the effects these or other objects of Masonry, including the compass and the square, have had on me or my family, in the name of Jesus Christ.

In the name and authority of Jesus Christ, I break every curse of Freemasonry in my life, including the curses of barrenness, sickness, mind-blinding and poverty, and I rebuke every evil spirit which empowered these curses.

I also renounce, cut off and dissolve in the blood of Jesus Christ every ungodly Soul-Tie I or my ancestors have created with other lodge members or participants in occultic groups and actions, and I ask you to send out ministering angels to gather together all portions of my fragmented soul, to free them from all bondages and to wash them clean in the Blood of Jesus Christ, and then to restore them to wholeness to their rightful place within me. I also ask that You remove from me any parts of any other person's soul which has been deposited within my humanity. Thank you Lord for restoring my soul and sanctifying my spirit.

I renounce and rebuke every evil spirit associated with Freemasonry, Witchcraft , the Occult and all other sins and iniquities. Lord Jesus, I ask you to now set me free from all spiritual and other bondages, in accordance with the many promises of the Bible.

In the name of the Lord Jesus Christ, I now take the delegated authority given to me and bind every spirit of sickness, infirmity, curse, affliction, addiction, disease or allergy associated with these sins I have confessed and renounced, including every spirit empowering all iniquities inherited from my family. I exercise the delegated authority from the Risen Lord Jesus Christ over all lower levels of evil spirits and demons which have been assigned to me, and I command that all such demonic beings are to be bound up into one, to be separated from every part of my humanity, whether perceived to be in the body or trapped in the dimensions, and they are not permitted to transfer power to any other spirits or to call for reinforcements.

I command, in the name of Jesus Christ, for every evil spirit to leave me now, touching or harming no-one, and go to the dry place appointed for you by the Lord Jesus Christ, never to return to me or my family, and I command that you now take all your memories, roots, scars, works, nests and habits with you. I surrender to God's Holy Spirit and to no other spirit all the places in my life where these sins and iniquities have been.

Conclusion

Holy Spirit, I ask that you show me anything else which I need to do or to pray so that I and my family may be totally free from the consequences of the sins of Masonry, Witchcraft, Mormonism and all related Paganism and Occultism.

(Pause, while listening to God, and pray as the
Holy Spirit leads you.)

Now, dear Father God, I ask humbly for the blood of Jesus Christ, your Son and my Saviour, to cleanse me from all these sins I have confessed and renounced, to cleanse my spirit, my soul, my mind, my emotions and every part of my body which has been affected by these sins, in the name of Jesus Christ. I also command every cell in my body to come into divine order now, and to be healed and made whole as they were designed to by my loving Creator, including restoring all chemical balances and neurological functions, controlling all cancerous cells, reversing all degenerative diseases, and I sever the DNA and RNA of any mental or physical diseases or afflictions that came down through my family blood lines. I also ask to receive the perfect love of God which casts out all fear, in the name of the Lord Jesus Christ.

I ask you, Lord, to fill me with your Holy Spirit now according to the promises in your Word. I take to myself the whole armour of God in accordance with Ephesians Chapter Six, and rejoice in its protection as Jesus surrounds me and fills me with His Holy Spirit. I enthrone you, Lord

Jesus, in my heart, for you are my Lord and my Saviour, the source of eternal life. Thank you, Father God, for your mercy, your forgiveness and your love, in the name of Jesus Christ, Amen."

Since the above is what needs to be renounced, why would anyone want to join?

This information is taken from *Unmasking Freemasonry – Removing the Hoodwink*, (ISBN 978-1877463-00-6) by Dr. Selwyn Stevens published by Jubilee Resource International Inc., PO Box 36-044, Wellington Mail Centre 5045, New Zealand.

Notice Copying of this prayer is both permitted and encouraged provided reference is made to Book title, Author, Publisher & web address – www.jubilee-resources.com. This and other similar prayers are available to download freely from our website. Resources on other subjects are also available to educate and equip Christians on a wide range of spiritual deceptions. These prayers are also in Spanish, Brazilian Portuguese, French, German and Italian, and other languages as can be arranged.

Additional Resources

Telling Yourself the Truth, William Backus, Ph.D., Bethany House Publishing 1985.

Who Am I and Why Am I Here, Dr. Bill Hamon, Destiny Image Publishing, 2005.

Activating You to Heal the Sick: Masterclass Workbook, Patti Hathaway, M.Ed., CSP, Breakthrough Hope & Healing, 2020.

I Don't Have to Make Everything All Better, Gary and Joy Lundberg, Penguin Books, 2000.

The Handbook for Spiritual Warfare, Dr. Ed Murphy, Thomas Nelson Publishers, 1992.

Healing the Wounded Spirit, John and Paula Sandford, Bridge Publishing, 1985.

Other Prayer Resources:

Freemasonry and other religions: https://jubileeresources. org/?page_id=86

Authority Prayers from Erin Lamb: https://ithoughtiknew-whatlovewas.com/authority-prayers/

Prayers from Rev. Annie Aakelian: http://lightofthecom-forter.org/prayers/

Ministry Resources

Patti Hathaway is a best-selling author and Certified Speaking Professional who has been speaking over 30 years in the corporate arena. Her Human Trafficking Awareness: W.A.R. on Slavery eLearning programs are cutting edge and transform how people think and behave with victims. She is ordained through Patricia King's Women in Ministry Network. Her anointing is in healing (body, soul, and spirit) and her ministry is called Breakthrough Hope & Healing. She's been a leader in several healing rooms.

Patti is an activator who encourages and emboldens others to be bold and confident in Jesus' strength, not their own. An author of 7 books and 6 eLearning programs, she is on the leadership team of Street Souldiers, where she collaborates and develops world changing strategies to transform the inner city, unify the church body, and bring God glory. Her latest book is: Activating You to Heal the Sick and a booklet Contend for Your Healing. Available on amazon.

Contact Patti Hathaway, M.Ed., CSP at GoHeal4God@protonmail.com; 614-523-3633 or 1-800-339-0973.

You can learn more about Patti at her websites:
www.BreakthroughHopeHealing.com
www.HumanTraffickingElearning.com
www.TheChangeAgent.com
www.StreetSouldiers.com

To obtain a list of learning resources, Breakthrough Biblical Counseling class schedule, upcoming conferences, and speaking engagements please visit our website at: www.breakthroughministries.org. Our Breakthrough Ministries phone number is 614-551-2263.

The Burkett's are available to minister in your church, organization, or speak at professional workshops and conferences. Their topics are not exclusive to counseling. They are well known nationally and internationally as dynamic speakers and ministers of the gospel.

Biblical Counseling Training is the core course the Burketts have taught for 36 years. The training includes five six-week modules. The purpose of the classes is to equip the saints to do the work of the ministry. Using biblical principles the modules are: Fundamentals of Biblical Counseling, Setting the Captives Free, Healing the Soul, Restoration of the Soul, Practicum (using the course tools in various pragmatic issues, and a practicum with the class students).

9 780990 476320